ANITHER
DASH O' DORIC

MORE WIT AND WISDOM OF THE NORTH-EAST

NORMAN HARPER
AND
ROBBIE SHEPHERD

ILLUSTRATED BY GRAHAM MACLENNAN

CANONGATE BOOKS

First published in Great Britain in 1996 by
Canongate Books Ltd
14 High Street
Edinburgh EH1 1TE

ISBN 0 86241 637 X

British Library Cataloguing in Publication Data

A catalogue record for this volume is available
on request.

Typeset by Palimpsest Book Production Limited,
Polmont, Stirlingshire
Printed and bound in Finland by W.S.O.Y.

Contents

Foreword

WHEN the two of us began discussions in the middle of 1995 to see if there was potential for a book of true stories to illustrate the humour of the North-east, we ran into a problem very quickly: it was difficult to keep the serious discussion on course as one or the other of us sidetracked the meeting by recalling tale after tale after tale as they popped into our heads. There was mair sidetrack nor strategy that first time, believe us.

So that opening meeting became more or less a story session, rather than any plan of attack. Even by the end of the second meeting, we still didn't have much of a strategy – but the pile of stories was building up nicely.

It took until the third or fourth meeting before we realised that we didn't need much of a strategy at all. If the two of us had been so tickled just by swapping these tales from our own pasts, wouldn't others in the North-east corner be just as amused? In other words, our strategy had developed under our noses without our even realising it.

Originally, we had a notion to split the stories into chapters covering the industries of the North-east. We saw chapters on the funny tales of fishing and farming and shipbuilding and granite and forestry, and so on.

Ah, but humour's nae that easy split.

Try as we might, some stories were thrawn enough to refuse to be jammed into one chapter or another, and so we hatched the idea of letting the stories accumulate and seeing how they wanted to be split themselves. Eventually, we came up with the format you'll have seen in *A Dash o' Doric*.

Neither of us was sure how the book would be received, or if it would sell at all outside the few hundred hard-core Doricists in country areas everywhere from Strathisla to Buchan to the Mearns. In fact, we had quite a stammygaster on the day of the launch when the two of us duly sat down at a table for a signing session at one of Aberdeen's top bookstores and didn't sign more than 40 books in the entire hour.

You can imagine how we were feeling as we hauled on our coats that Saturday and left the shop. After six months of discussion and work, we had produced a stinker. We were almost inconsolable. Our wives, Esma and Alison, told us to buck up our ideas and have faith. Norman went to have a stiff lemonade. Robbie favoured a large Maccie and water.

What we didn't know was that the launch had not been advertised properly and that virtually no one had known that the book existed, save for those few hardy souls braving the Union Street pre-Christmas gales who had happened to see the wee poster and display of books in the shop window.

It wasn't until the following Wednesday that we had an inkling of what was to follow. The deputy manager of the bookshop called the *Press and Journal* to say: 'Just to lift your spirits after the signing session, I thought you'd like to hear that suddenly everybody seems to know about *A Dash o' Doric*. The books are just flying out of the shop. People are buying them in twos, threes and fours. One woman bought twelve. We can hardly keep up. We've ordered another thousand, but we don't think we can get them quickly enough. We're taking bets among the staff in the shop as to which book will be our Christmas Number One, and the smart money's on *A Dash o' Doric*.'

Three days later, *A Dash o' Doric* was at Number One, where it stayed for a record eight weeks. It was Christmas Number One, New Year Number One and was still in the North-east charts the following March.

After the second reprint, Canongate decided to try the book in the rest of Scotland. Neither of us was particularly confident about that, for one region's humour doesn't travel well. In fact, the book began selling throughout the rest of Scotland to such an extent that now, a year after its launch, it is still in the Scottish Top 10.

Now, in case you think we're telling you all this to be bigsy, we're certainly not. But it does illustrate what both of us have said for years: that nothing fascinates fowk as much as their own culture, their own language – in fact, themselves. And the great thing about the North-east is that we have a rare ability to laugh at ourselves.

So that is why *A Dash o' Doric* has done so well. It has very little to do with the two of us, and a'thing to do with you, the reader, and your devotion to your heritage. If we've been able to help that along, we're delighted.

In light of all that, it has also made *Anither Dash o' Doric* inevitable.

As before, we're indebted to everyone who has written to us with stories from their pasts – particularly exiles around the world who wrote nice things about the first book and about how it sparked memories and, on occasions, hamesickness. The book wouldn't be the same without the breadth of stories that you have shared with us.

But we thought we'd leave you with two examples of Doric humour, so fresh they're still rikkin, which come directly from our launch activities last year.

When any new book goes on the market, the publisher likes the author/s to do a wee tour, so the two of us came to be stravaigin round bookshops everywhere from Elgin to Aberdeen during November and December last year.

At Inverurie, we were duly signing books and hearing stories from people who were kind enough to come and meet us. There was a lull in the proceedings about halfway through, when two elderly ladies who had just had their books signed were making their way to the door and studying our signatures on the inside of the jacket. We heard one say to the other: 'Of coorse, that Norman Harper, he's a lot auler nor he maks himsel oot ti be.'

And at Fraserburgh, we had just finished for the evening

and the last of the customers were being shown from the premises when we overheard one elderly woman say to another: 'Weel, I fair enjoyed that, bit I'm rale worried aboot Robbie Shepherd. I nivver kent he'd sic an affa reed face.'

Thanks to all of them and to you for buying the book. We hope you enjoy it as much as Number One, and as much as we enjoyed putting it together.

Haste ye back.

Robbie Shepherd and Norman Harper
Aberdeen, 1996

Babes and Sucklings

Some of the best humour from any part of the world spills from the mouths of children. That's as true of the North-east as anywhere, as this selection proves.

THE LATE Betty Watson, of Ordhead, Cluny, was a Sunday School teacher in the district and was telling her class the story of how Pharaoh's daughter found the baby Moses floating in a basket among the bullrushes.

A young laddie's voice piped up: 'Aye, that wis her story.'

AT THE same Sunday School at Cluny, to see if they had been paying attention, Miss Watson started asking questions and when asking what an epistle was was given the answer:

'Is't apostle's wife?'

YVONNE CORMACK lived at Aboyne in the mid-1970s and recalls an evening of one of the fiercest thunder-and-lightning storms she had experienced. She was nervous enough for herself, but she was concerned that her six-year-old, Christopher, tucked safely upstairs in bed, would be beside himself with terror.

Yvonne made her way upstairs and, flinching between cracks of thunder and flashes of lightning, listened outside Christopher's room. She could hear a small voice from inside the bedroom, but couldn't make out what he was saying.

As quietly as she could, she opened the door to find Christopher standing on top of the small toy chest in front of the bedroom window, curtains opened, eyes wide with excitement and clapping his hands and squealing with delight:

'Bang it again, God. Bang it again.'

LATER, WHEN Christopher was a year older, and Yvonne became pregnant with her second child, she sat Christopher down and explained what was happening. With a very serious look on his face, he considered all the implications.

Then Yvonne added: 'So I doot we'll hae ti move hoose, Christopher.'

Christopher looked up: 'Will the baby nae folly us and find oot far we are?'

AS A CHILD, Margaret Mathison, of Edinburgh, spent her summer holidays in a Banffshire fishing town, where one of her playmates lived with her granny. Granny had brought up the entire family, but always welcomed Margaret into her home for a chat.

The oldest grand-daughter had moved South to go into service and, in due course, had wed and had given birth to a son.

Margaret happened to visit on the day the baby arrived at great-grandma's home for the first time.

'Did ye ken that oor Jeannie's gotten a loonie?' enquired the new great-grandma.

'Oh, that's good news,' said Margaret.

'And div ye ken fit she's ca'ed him?' said great-grandma.

'No.'

'She's ca'ed him Keith.'

'Oh,' said Margaret.

'Gweed sakes,' said great-grandma with a dry snort of disapproval, 'she micht as weel hiv ca'ed him Fochabers.'

A KEITH teacher was told by one of her infant class that he had a new baby brother. 'Oh, how super,' she said, 'and what's he called?'

'Spot.'

'Spot? That's a strange name. Are you sure?'

'Spot,' repeated the boy firmly.

It wasn't until a few days later, when she met the

'Fit's she ca'ed him?'

newborn's mother in town, that the mystery was cleared up.

The baby's name was Mark.

JESS ROBERTSON, now of Dundee, recalls her son, David, going back to Oldmeldrum Primary School after the summer holidays and stepping up from Primary Two to Primary Three.

When he returned home after his first day, Jess asked him how things had been and if he had liked his new teacher.

'She wis the same as the last een,' he said. 'Jist a different heid.'

MELISSA WAS fascinated with the news that the young couple next door had had a baby boy, and phoned her grandma at Inverurie to tell her the news.

'That's good news, Melissa,' said Grandma. 'And fit are they ca'in him?'

Melissa hesitated for a moment, then said: 'Chewed. They're ca'in him Chewed.'

'Chewed?'

'Chewed.'

Only later did Grandma discover that the problem had arisen because Melissa's mum insisted on the Queen's English at all times and didn't want her drifting into the Doric.

The baby's name was Chad.

DAVID RETURNED home from his first day back at school at Mintlaw Primary and his mother was anxious to know how he had got on.

'Fit did ye learn, David?'

'Nithing.'

'Ye must hiv learned something.'

'Well, the wifie wintit ti ken foo ti spell HORSE, so I jist telt her and she didna bother me efter 'at.'

YOUNG MICHAEL was definitely his father's son. Only five, he strode about the farm with his wee chestie puffed out, thumbs in the straps of his specially made dungars, eyeing up the nowt and sitting with the farm labourers at fly time.

Eventually there came an addition to the family, a baby sister, and Michael's aunt from Aberdeen asked him if he was pleased with the new baby.

'Fairly that,' he said, scowling as he hauled off his wee wellies. 'Though we'd mair need o a new ploo.'

KENNETHMONT HALL was the scene of a fiddlers' recital one evening in the early 1970s. A fair number of children had been brought along, for these were the days before childminders and babysitters.

Evidently, fiddle music wasn't quite the cup of tea of one young man, for during the first fiddle solo, his voice floated across the crowd:

'Mam, dis he stop fin he cuts his box in twa?'

WE TAKE you to a geography lesson in a school where it was frowned upon to use the mither tongue. Only standard English was acceptable.

Doris Bruce, of Montrose, taught in Muirfield Primary School in Aberdeen some 35 years ago. She discovered that her Primary Five pupils knew nothing about the Channel Isles, so she decided on a little lesson there and then.

A few days later, Miss Bruce asked: 'Now, who can remember the names of some of those islands?'

Well, she got Jersey and Guernsey and then they stuck.

At last, a lass who never said much put up her hand. 'Please, miss,' she started. 'Sh-sh-sh-sh', and then she halted with a sudden look of horror.

'Yes, Elizabeth?'

'Shirt.'

ALL THE way from Victoria, Australia, came this reminder of early school days back home, from Norah Hardy.

At the beginning of one term, a poor wee chap turned up all on his own for his very first day at school. Of course, he had to be registered.

'What's your name?'

'Jimmy Gordon.'

'What's your father's name?'

'I dinna ken.'

'Well, what does your mother call him?'

'A coorse bugger.'

THE PUPILS at Rayne North School were asked if they knew any poems by Robert Burns. Elsie stood up and started to recite:

'Wee sleekit, coorin, timrous beastie

'Oh, what a bannock's in thy breastie.'

ETHEL BAIRD, of Kincorth, tells of visiting a neighbour to see the new baby and finding four-year-old Robert sitting on the sofa in the front room with a face like thunder.

'Are ye prood o yer new baby brither, Robert?' she enquired.

But Robert said nothing.

'Fa div ye think he's like?'

Still nothing.

'I wid say he's got yer dad's nose and yer mither's een.'

'Aye,' said Robert, 'and he's got my bedroom.'

Sweet Bird of Doric Wit

By the time they leave childhood, North-east teenagers are well schooled in the ways of the mither tongue, as these few examples demonstrate.

A LETTER from Donald McAllister, of Banff, reported that his son, Derek, now a happily married man with a grown-up family, was a beatnik (or as close as Banff could manage) in the 1960s, with all the paraphernalia of Beatlemania – the shaggy haircut, tight trousers, steel comb and Mini Traveller passionwagon.

He and his friends had decided to go for a week's holiday to London, presumably to enhance their wardrobes in Carnaby Street and to do the rounds of the clubs.

After a few tinctures one evening, they had tumbled out of a club, high on John Barleycorn, and had fallen straight at the feet of a London bobby.

The bobby watched as they picked themselves up and calmed themselves down then, studying their winklepickers, asked with a mild hint of a sneer: 'Do your feet really fit those shoes?'

'Aye,' said Derek. 'Dis your heid really fit that hat?'

HOME FROM Edinburgh University, Donna Hendry, of Banchory, noticed that her grandmother, who lived with the family, had taken a sudden notion for reading the Bible, and every spare minute was spent with her nose in the good book.

Donna's mother had also noticed and, she tells us, mentioned the fact to Donna.

'Dinna worry aboot it,' said Donna reassuringly. 'She's jist studyin for her finals.'

DURING THE war, when many a raw young North-east loon found himself in the deserts of North Africa, a sergeant

with the background of Perwinnes rather than the Pyrenees
was drilling his men near the pyramids of Egypt and was
frustrated to find that the young squaddies' eyes kept
wandering towards the monuments.

Eventually, the sergeant lost his rag.

'Fit the hell are ye glowerin at?' he bawled. 'A rickle o
aul steens. His neen o ye seen Bennachie?'

NEGLECT THE perspective of the bairns of the North-east
at your peril. They're taking in everything to store for future
use when the occasion arises.

Jimmy Glennie, of Inverurie, told of the lad watching the
morning ritual in the bathroom before the day's work had
really begun. He enquired: 'Dad, fit wye's yer hair makkin
that cracklin soon?'

'That's the electric comin aff fin I comb it.'

A wee while later, he spotted his mother.

'Mam, fit wye's yir belly makkin at queer soon?'

'Must be something I've aeten. Jist a bittie gas.'

Next day, the lad was playing outside with his pal whose
parents were doing rather well from the work in the oil
industry and the five-year-old son of the rigger wasn't slow
in coming forward to say so.

'My dad's got plenty money. They're jist back fae a
holiday in Hong Kong.'

There was a moment's hesitation and a moment's jeal-
ousy until our young hero brightened:

'That's nithing; my dad's got electric in his heid and ma
mam's got gas in her belly.'

AN INFORMED source – a retired Garioch teacher who
sought anonymity – recalled overhearing two young lads
who were discussing the forthcoming school play in which
one of them had to kiss the heroine.

'I've nivver tried es kissin afore,' confided one to the
other. 'Fit wye div ye dee't?'

'It's easy,' said one. 'Jist steek yer moo lik ye wis sookin a pandrop.'

CHARLES BARRON, Arts Director of the Haddo Arts Trust, told us of his days as a young teacher at Inverurie Academy and being landed last thing on a Friday with a difficult class 1S.

They were not the most academically gifted, and one Friday, as in the previous three or four weeks, he had been hammering home gender equivalents. For example, the female form of master is mistress; the female form of ram is ewe, and so on.

Sandy was a richt fine loon, but always the slowest of the class at answering.

However, this Friday, Charles came to the female equivalent of duke and, to his astonishment, Sandy's hand went up.

Face flushed with excitement, hair standing on end with effort, Sandy delivered his answer with all the confidence of the man who knows, beyond all question, that he is right.

'Drake,' he said. 'A wifie deuk's a drake.'

IT MIGHT have been three of the same lads who were asked in another Inverurie Academy class to name the odd man out among potato, cabbage and knife.

'Knife,' said the first. 'The ither twa's veggies.'

'Knife,' said the second. 'It's the only een wi metal in't.'

'Cubbidge,' said the third.

'Cabbage?' said the teacher. 'How do you work that out?'

'Ye can mak chips wi the ither twa.'

DURING A school inspection at an Aberdeenshire academy in the early 1960s, the inspector sat down beside a 14-year-old and began discussing his work and looking at the books in his desk.

Eventually, during a lull in proceedings, the boy got up and asked his teacher who the man was. She explained that he was a schools inspector and that the boy should answer whatever questions were put to him.

He went back to his desk, sat for a while, then asked for permission to go out to the basket to sharpen his pencil. After a while, his teacher said: 'Now, you've been sharpening that pencil long enough. You can go back to your desk.'

'I canna,' he whispered.

'Why not?'

'Yon detective's still at it. He's surely lookin for clues.'

WHILE WORKING for the co-opie butcher in his youth, Donald Manson was put to making sausages. He declares himself appalled at what went into them and, worse still, at one point he stumbled while carrying sawdust and some of the sawdust went into the mixture waiting to go into the skins.

'I went, trembling, to the boss,' wrote Donald. 'I said: "I've drappit saadust in the sassidges, I'm soarry." '

'Na, na,' soothed the boss. 'There's nithing lik an improved recipe.'

JAMES MORRISON, now of Urybank, recalls his days as a fee'd loon and attending the dances in the old distillery at Jericho, near Colpy. The band was put at one end of a loft so long that the music could barely be heard at the other end.

The loft was reached by a set of stone stairs outside – without railings, of course.

Charlie Nicol and Doug Allardyce were two fairm loons who liked a dram. One dance night, they had a fair whack o the barley-bree and, when they decided to go home, Charlie led the way.

But Charlie forgot about the stair and stepped over the

side, fell off the top and landed on his back in a bed of nettles.

He was so anaesthetised that he was not badly hurt – just stung all over – but, anxious that his pal didn't meet the same fate, he raised his head and shouted:

'Doug! Watch that first step! She's a bugger!'

Kissies and Bosies

The North-east's romantic attachments are no different from anywhere else's, except that we don't talk about them as much. Perhaps these few examples will explain why.

STRAE-RICK fun and frolics involving Elsie and Dode, from two small villages in Banffshire, had led to Elsie's *condition*, although Dode denied it vehemently.

A week after the birth, Elsie's family called a meeting to resolve the matter. On Elsie's side were mother, father and a host of glowering relatives. The only support Dode could muster was his steadfast, loyal younger brother, Wullie.

According to our informant, Wullie was a smiling, open-faced taakin kine o a loon, willing to perjure himself completely in Dode's defence. Why, had the two of them not been in each other's company miles and miles away from the alleged romps on the evening in question.

Alas for Dode.

Steadfast brother Wullie took one look at the innocent in the pram, beamed at the little smiling facie, then turned sadly to Dode and said:

'Oh, Dode, ye canna deny that.'

BILL MOWAT turned up at his Peterhead local with his arm in a sling. The regulars looked him up and down and demanded to know how the accident had happened.

'If ye must ken,' said Bill, 'it got broke fechtin for a lassie's honour.'

'Is that so?'

'Aye, she wintit ti keep it.'

FROM DONSIDE comes the tale of a family who travelled en masse in 1990 to the Leicestershire wedding of one of the young men of their family, who had fallen in love with the English sweetheart he had met at university there.

The wedding was a fairly lavish affair (marquees on the lawn, vol-au-vents, horse-drawn landaulettes – that sort of thing) because, after all, the bride's family was paying. Not only that, but the bride and her family had requested that the ceremony and service be conducted as a 12th-century Eucharist. The obscurity leant it even more elan.

Our Donsiders felt a little out of their depth and, anxious not to show up their boy, had decided to say as little as possible. They had also warned their eight-year-old daughter, something of a tomboy, that discipline would be swift and merciless if she stepped out of line.

Ranks of guests in their finery filled every available pew, and they spanned the entire age spectrum, from grisly matriarchs scowling about them; to rosy-cheeked, avuncular men; to snuffly, emotional mothers, aunties and sisters, and to a brace of under-10s, obviously warned to be on their best behaviour.

There sat the children, faces scrubbed and shining; hair slicked and styled to impossible perfection, dangling their little feet and scarcely concealing their boredom.

A hush fell on the congregation as the organ music died away and the ceremony began. Solemn words echoed to the magnificent rococo ceilings. As the vows were taken, hankies began appearing quietly in various pews.

The couple knelt before the vicar for the blessing, and the silence thickened until it was almost unbearable. It was punctuated only by a very small, impatient North-east voice demanding:

'Is this fin he pits his pollen in her?'

OUR INFORMANT wasn't able to provide hard evidence, but she said with an admirably straight face that a fund-raising cookbook for a notable Buchan church contains the line:

'Many people are obsessed with turnips, and I am married to one.'

Beauty is in the eye of the beholder

AGGIE AND Sandy, from a craftie not a million miles from Lonmay, had been together 45 years when Sandy retired from his life as a farm-worker. It was to be a big upheaval for Sandy, who was set in his ways. The same would have applied, presumably, to Aggie, having been left on her own for most of the days.

A neighbour ventured to ask as to how she was looking forward to retirement.

'Ach,' she said, 'it'll jist mean twice as muckle o the man and half the siller.'

WE'RE INDEBTED to Duncan Downie, of Kemnay, for this one.

In the village, there lived a well-known spinster by the name of Suffie. We go back to the days when gas lamps were the standard lighting on the bicycles that took you everywhere – especially to village dances at night.

To get a click, it was a ploy of the local belles to ask the lad of their fancy if he had a light to get her gas lamp going. Alas, not for Suffie, as she moaned realistically:

'Plenty spunks. Nivver a lad.'

JIM McCOLL, of Beechgrove Garden fame, contributed this wee gem. The village in question was overloaded with licensed premises and so the publicans had to use their wits to see which one could attract the most business.

Round the village went the rumour that Airchie was seeking planning permission for a nightclub, complete with scantily dressed models.

Annie and Maggie got claikin.

'I hear it said that Airchie's applyin for change o use til a brothel.'

'Michty, Annie, if he canna mak siller sellin drink, he'll nae mak it sellin soup.'

WE'RE NOW in the picture house at Ballater in the late 1940s, and there's a young couple in the back row. It was the time that the travelling cinema shows toured the country areas with such black-and-white epics as *Laurel and Hardy in Bonnie Scotland* and the continuing sagas of *Flash Gordon*.

From the back row, there came this conversation.

'Div ye still love me, Wullie?'

'Aye. I still love ye.'

'Are ye sure ye still love me, Wullie?'

'Aye, I'm sure I still love ye, Jeannie.'

'Fit wye div ye nivver tell me ye love me, Wullie?'

'Look, I really love ye, a'richt?'

'Wullie, if ye still really love me, fit wye div ye nivver ficher wi me noo?'

TAM AND Kirstie lived in a remote glen round about Tomintoul. Every evening, as young lovers did, Tam came to call and they would go for a walk up the glen. This daily ritual had gone on for 14 years, but there was still no word of matrimony.

So it was on this particular evening that the moon was full and the air warm and soft – a night just made for lovers. And Kirstie, as they say, 'fell from grace'.

Returning down the glen, not a word was spoken, but when they reached the gate of her cottage, Kirstie could contain herself no longer. 'Tam,' she said in a voice filled with emotion. 'Ye'll be thinkin I'm jist a common hooer.'

Clearly alarmed, Tam replied: 'Na, na, Kirstie, there wis nivver ony mention o siller.'

AUL DODDIE, who stayed on a craftie near Muir of Fowlis in the mid-Sixties, was enjoying a dram with his cronies in the lounge of the Muggarthaugh Hotel discussing, among other things, the merits of a shapely young customer, resplendent in a micro mini-skirt.

Noticing the fair bit of attention Doddie was giving the exposed thighs, the proprietor asked what was going through his mind.

'I wis jist thinkin,' said Doddie, 'that fin the Gweed Lord taen awa the ability, fit wye did he nae tak awa the inclination?'

IT WAS the night of the Lonach Gathering, and the Colquhonnie Hotel was fully booked as far as bedrooms were concerned, and fair bursting at the seams with the day's revellers.

All appeared quiet on lights-out an hour or two after last orders, and the homeless stragglers were offered a shak-doon in the residents' lounge.

One particular young lady had been the life and soul of the party and had much impressed the young, hot-blooded lads o Lonach, who now found they shared the same accommodation.

Now resting in deep sleep draped over the settee, our temptress and husband lay to full exposure. One lad more adventurous than the others fancied he would give her a goodnight bosie.

The restless husband stirred, saw the attention of the young chiel and said: 'Hey min, it's me that dis the interficherin roon here.'

DUNCAN DOWNIE, of Kemnay, told of characters in his village, principally two sisters, Mary and Sophia Adam. Both were single and Mary predeceased Suffie by a few years.

Mr Downie Sen. called with his taxi to collect Suffie one evening to go visiting and, as she came out of the house door, she just pulled it shut behind her and didn't bother locking up. Mr Downie drew her attention to what he thought was an oversight.

'Are ye nae lockin yer door?'

'I nivver lock ma door,' replied Suffie.

'Are ye nae feart ye'll find some mannie in the hoose fin ye come back?'

'Nivver been sae lucky.'

JOHN DUFF tells of the Braemar father who watched as his daughter's new boyfriend turned up at the house to take her to a village dance. As they turned to go, he warned the boy: 'Noo dinna blaad the lassie.'

The Shoppie

One of the advantages of Sunday shopping must be that it increases by one-sixth the time available for that peculiar brand of humour that lives on both sides of the counters and up and down the aisles of all manner of North-east emporia.

IN THE early 1970s, when the North-east was gripped with freezer fever, it became fashionable to buy beef in bulk.

One Turriff carnivore phoned Johnny Stewart, the Portsoy butcher, to inquire about freezer packs.

After all the essentials about quantities, cuts and price had been sorted out, the Turriff man asked: 'And do you deliver?'

'Michty, aye,' replied the butcher. 'We dee a' kinds o beef.'

MARY GERRIE had promised her grandson a computer for his eighteenth birthday if he managed to gain acceptance to university. Realising she had better price a few computers in case he succeeded in his part of the bargain, she took herself along to a store in Union Street, Aberdeen and, completely out of her depth with technology, began scouting round the computer section.

Having perused all the price tags, she spied one which she thought looked nacky and began pushing a few buttons to see what it would do. All she could get out of it was a high-pitched beeping.

Eventually, a salesman hurried across and asked her, rather abruptly, what she was doing.

'I've promised ma grandson a computer for his birthday,' she said, 'and I canna get this thing ti work ata.'

'Jist as weel,' said the salesman. 'That's wir till.'

'Do you dee liver?'

THE SCENE was Asda, Dyce, and a harassed young mum Karen Buchan, from Fyvie, had turned up on a busy Saturday morning with two pre-school children in tow to do the monthly shop.

Halfway round, Karen noticed that she was being followed very closely by an elderly gentleman. Whenever she turned into another aisle, he turned into the aisle. Whenever she picked up speed, he picked up speed.

Since you can never be too careful, Karen decided that she had better find a member of staff and had just spotted a shelf-stacker when the elderly gentleman finally caught up with her and stopped her. Karen felt a flash of panic.

'Excuse me,' he said, mildly out of breath. 'Wid it be OK if I got ma trolley back?'

AS DISCUSSED in Volume One, Bessie and Maggie were two Alford spinsters, now sadly deceased, who lived a spartan existence on the eastern edge of the howe.

Once a week, Bessie would arrive at the Whitehouse Shop and shove a tray or two of eggs at the shopkeeper. He would inspect them; they would agree a price, and Bessie would ram the money into the pocket of her coat and leave.

Now and again, the shopkeeper would scan the eggs and say jokingly: 'Aye, Bessie, yer eggs is nae affa clean the day.'

And a sharp, wiry hand would shoot out from the coat, snatch an egg and hold it up close to her glasses for inspection.

The result was always the same. Bessie would lick the egg, spit on it, rub it up and down the lapel of her coat and ram it back into the cardboard tray and stare sharply at the grocer, defying him to find any more fault with her produce.

He never did.

ONCE, BESSIE happened to bump into a customer who knew the provenance of the duck's eggs. 'Excuse me, Bessie,' said the customer, 'bit I believe you supply the Whitehoose Shop wi dyeuck eggs?'

'I div that,' said Bessie.

'Well, I'm sorry ti say that I hid een recently and it wis rotten.'

'Ach,' said Bessie with a dismissive wave of the hand. 'Canna dee nithing aboot that. That wis the wye the dyeuck laid it.'

NOW WE turn to the art of coiffeur, although in certain parts of the North-east the short back and sides is still referred to as a 'bowl crop'.

Doug Argo, a weel-kent farmer from the Howe o the Mearns, was in need of a haircut and, being a busy man, had not too much time to spare.

In he went to his local barber at Edzell where – changed days – a young lady would attend to the surplus of thatch.

Doug sat himself down and was soon lost in his own thoughts of the day ahead.

Snip snip went the shears until the young lady said something which our Douglas barely heard above the birr of the machine.

'Oh,' replied Doug, 'aboot half wye atween Fettercairn and Auchenblae.'

Our farmer friend thought that she had said: 'Where do you do your farming?'

No wonder the young hairdresser doubled up in laughter; what she had actually said was:

'Where do you have your parting?'

THE YEAR was 1934 and J.O. McHardy had just been promoted to grocer's vanman, entrusted with the 1922 Model T Ford.

This elevation saw him in all kinds of weather, taking in the whole countryside around Wardhouse of Insch.

In the spring of the following year, there was a glut of hens' eggs and, with the guile of which country folk are bred, the decision was made to buy for nothing more than 'saxpince the dizzen'.

J.O. set out on his Friday run which took in, as usual, the farm of Sleepytoun.

The farmer's wife, a good-hearted soul, was told the price being offered for her eggs and replied:

'Laddie, it's nae worth the craters raxin for't.'

BAIRNS AT Woodside, Aberdeen, made sure that the route to the corner shoppie was well used. Bargains were to be had, of course, and aul Andra, the shopkeeper, aye had a pocketful of rather grubby pandrops to entice the youngsters on to other wares.

The handing-over of the pandrop was always accompanied by:

'Jist spit oot the first sook.'

ON A visit to Strathdon, Ian Middleton, from near Buckie, went into the shop and asked for a new type of chocolate bar he had seen advertised on TV.

'Could I hae a Topic, please?' he inquired, to which he got the answer:

'Affa sorry, loon. I've jist the Dandy and the Beano.'

ACCORDING TO our informant, Granny took young Tracy to shop for a wedding gift at Makro, the Dutch-owned wholesale superstore newly set-up in Aberdeen. She made for the crystal display and was taken with a rosebowl complete with silver mesh.

'This'll dee, I'm sure,' said Granny, keeping the youngster occupied.

'Oh I ken fit at's for, Grunny,' said Tracy.
'Fit?' said Granny, wondering what was coming.
'Breein cubbidge.'

Doon on the Fairm

The sons and daughters of the land are the backbone of North-east humour, as anyone who has spent a morning at any North-east mart can testify.

BUNKIE PETRIE, a celebrated Aberdeenshire farmer, used to tell a story of two farmers at the old Alford mart taking everyone and everything through haun when an extremely glamorous young woman, dolled up to the nines and made up and bejewelled most elegantly, strolled into the mart building, obviously for a look at how the other half lived.

'Michty,' said one farmer to the other. 'Fit wid ye dee wi a deemie lik that?'

His companion surveyed her with the steady eye of Aberdeenshire farming stock.

'Na, Bill,' he said. 'If it needs a' that tap-dressin, it maun be gey sair grun aneth.'

BUCHAN MEAT, one of the great farming organisations of Scotland, had a rocky 1996, suffering great financial uncertainty, partly to do with the BSE crisis. There was one little glimmer of North-east humour at a creditors' meeting, attended by farmers and shareholders from throughout Buchan and beyond.

One journalist assigned to cover the meeting was growing more and more anxious about the likely finishing time because he had another pressing engagement. He turned to the chap standing next to him and whispered:

'Excuse me, but have you any idea what time this meeting might finish?'

The chap whispered back in broad Buchan: 'Ten ti fower.'

Since the meeting at that stage looked to be reaching its angry pitch, and it was already 3.35 p.m., the journalist was puzzled by the certainty and precision.

'That's very precise,' he whispered back. 'How can you be so sure?'

The helpful chap pointed across the assembly to a lone figure in dungars and requisite farmer's bunnet. 'Ye see that chiel ower there?' he said. 'That's Dode. Dode starts his milkin at fower.'

RETIRED KEITH vet John Dear told of the day, shortly after his arrival from Hampshire in 1961, when he was called out to see a sow with a problem. When he asked the old-lady smallholder what was the difficulty, she said: 'Ma soo's nae takkin her mate.'

Mr Dear began discussing possible fertility problems and wondered whether or not the sow was being presented properly to the boar.

The old woman glared at him and said: 'No, no, no. She's nae takkin her *maet*. Her maet. She's nae *aetin*.'

MR DEAR also told of an incident at the other end of his career, not long before his retirement, when he was called to a farmer who had reported several head of cattle with several sore eyes, or one beast with one sore eye, it was not quite clear from the phone message.

When he arrived, Mr Dear asked the farmer about the scale of the problem. Was it several eyes, or just one?

'Oh, aye,' said the farmer. 'Ae ee, aye.'

A RETIRED Maud farmer wrote to tell us of one of his neighbours, who had wed late in life and had supposedly proposed to his bride by saying:

'Is it nae aboot time you an me startit pittin wir teeth in ae cup?'

CHARLIE CHEYNE, who was a mechanic at an agricultural garage in the Howe of Alford in the 1960s and

'Fit wid ye dee wi a deemie lik that?'

1970s, used to tell of a farmer's teenage son who turned up one morning with one of the farm tractors looking for an emergency repair. Charlie downed tools to help the lad out and, while Charlie worked, the lad gabbed on and on, mostly about himself, the family farm and all the plans he had for it once his father retired.

'Aye,' said Charlie from the depths of the tractor, 'ye've great dreams surely.'

'Aye, Charlie,' said the lad, brimful of confidence and certainty. 'I dream I'll mak a million poun, jist lik the aul man.'

Charlie stopped. 'Yer faither nivver made a million poun,' he said.

'No,' said the lad, 'bit he's aye dreamin o't.'

DURING THE building of Thainstone Mart, near Inverurie, two Garioch farmers had stopped on their way back from Kittybrewster one Friday to see how construction was going and spotted a group of labourers gathered round watching two of their colleagues laying pipes.

'Look at that,' said Westie, 'ye widna hiv seen that thirty-forty year ago. In my day, the ganger let them lay twa length o pipe, then he turned on the watter. If they didna keep in front o't, they got the sack.'

THE LATE Maitland Mackie, a leading light in North-east local government in his day, used to tell of meeting an Echt farmer during a council site visit and getting newsing about the state of farming, before discovering that they had a mutual farmer acquaintance. The acquaintance's son had had a gweed heid on him, they had agreed, and had been expected to do great things as a doctor or lawyer or some such, but had ended up as a sewerage foreman for the old Aberdeen County Council.

There was a long silence while the two of them considered the lad's choice of career then, said Maitland, the farmer stood up from the fence on which he had been leaning and said: 'Weel, nivver mind, at least he can say he's Number One in Number Two.'

THE FARMER at Balblair was visited by a rather pushy salesman who was determined to sell him a fire-extinguisher.

'It's the latest model and guaranteed for five years. It's absolutely essential for anyone who is concerned about fire safety on his premises.'

'No.'

'For a very small investment you can have absolute peace of mind and be free to concentrate on other things.'

'No.'

'All forward-thinking farmers are realising that with so many flammable materials round the farm, a reliable fire extinguisher is essential these days.'

'No.'

'B-but what would you do if you had a fire and you didn't have one of our extinguishers?'

'Pish on't.'

IN THE early days of deep-litter hens, Jock Anderson had decided to give the new system a try. Bumping into him one day, his fairmer pal Doug Archibald asked how the hens were doing.

'Nae layin worth a damn. I'm nae happy wi them. I'm takkin them aff o the pellets – ower damnt dear. I'll try a mash o bruised corn and sma tatties.'

Seeing Jock a few weeks later, Doug was anxious to know how the hens were laying on their new diet.

'Nae worth a bugger,' said Jock. 'Nithing bit barrafaes o shite.'

A FARMER from Newburgh who was a most infrequent member of the village golf club was persuaded by a major fertiliser company to be a guest for a day's outing to St. Andrews.

The main hazards at Newburgh were only whin bushes, and he was totally unprepared for the obstacles awaiting him at the home of golf. Visiting one of the notorious bunkers out of sight of his partners, he was in deep trouble.

A plaintive cry went out after he had been in the same sand trap for about 10 minutes: 'Help. I canna win oot.'

'Ach,' said his playing partner waiting impatiently up the fairway, 'it's just a friendly. Throw the ball out and nobody will notice.'

'The ba? The ba? It's *me* that canna win oot.'

IT WAS the same player who, not adhering to the once-bitten-twice-shy maxim, joined yet another firm's outing, this time to Stonehaven. He came to the nasty ravine over the sea cliffs which is a nightmare for non-golfers. It's only a matter of 120 yards, but from the tee you are required to float the ball over the ravine to the small green at the other side.

Geordie sent one off and it went straight down the cliffs. Then another. And another. And another.

Losing patience completely, he took yet another new ball and set it on the tee still with the wrapper on.

There went another almighty swing with the parting words: 'Tak that, ye bugger. It's nae worth ma file takkin ye oot o the paper.'

A FARMER from Glenkindie was called into the tax office to explain certain deficiencies in his submitted accounts.

The inspector behind the desk said that he wasn't too pleased about his books and queried the fact that although the farmer had lots of cows, there was no record of any milk money.

'What do you do with the milk?' he asked.

'Oh,' said the farmer, 'I sook ma coos.'

'Don't be ridiculous,' snapped the taxman. 'How do you do that?'

'Ye bliddy feel, it's nae me that sooks the coos,' said the farmer. 'It's the caafies.'

DOUG HAMPTON, of Laurencekirk, reminded us of the plans to build a gents' toilet in the Lang Toon in the Thirties. The town paper referred to it as a urinal – a gey uncommon title for the watterie in those days.

At a heckling meeting prior to the district elections, a town worthy known only as Auld Dod got to his feet to ask: 'Far are ye gaun ti pit this arsenal abody's spikkin aboot?'

ANOTHER NOTABLE from the Laurencekirk area, Davie, had a dairy and floating business up beside the Western Hotel. He had about ten cows in the dairy and delivered milk around the town.

He decided it might be more economical to buy a bull and managed to procure a gey old beast, but good enough to sire his cows.

Davie took the first of the calves down to the mart hoping for a good price. When one was introduced to the ring as his, he realised there had been a mix-up.

'That's nae my calf,' he declared, much to the auctioneer's annoyance. Davie, the auctioneer and the mart manager convened a hasty meeting, and the manager insisted that the calf had to be Davie's, for his mart never made mistakes.

Glowering at the auctioneer, Davie shouted: 'Gweed God, I shid ken ma ain calf. I bulled the coo masel.'

A MEARNS farmer who was a bit of a blaw and some bothered with a thirst (so we won't name him because his descendants still farm in the area) was up at the Feein Market in the Castlegate, Aberdeen, during the 1914–18 war. As was the custom, the recruiting sergeants were buzzing around and a few of the lads were home on leave.

A Salvation Army lass came up to our Man o the Mearns with a collecting tin, to which he responded: 'Fit army are you in, then?'

'The Army of the Lord,' was the lass's reply.

'Weel, ye're a helluva lang wye fae yer barracks.'

IT WAS a National Farmers' Union meeting. Airchie was deaf and was missing most of the content of the speeches.

'Is that mannie aye spikkin?' he bawled into his neighbour's ear.

'Aye, he's aye spikkin,' came the weary reply. 'Bit he's nae sayin onything.'

AUL WILLIE stayed by himself and farmed his land single-handedly. He had his own system of home economics. A neighbour happened in past and, seeing the clutter on the mantelpiece, asked politely how Willie dealt with paying his bills.

'Ach,' said Willie. 'Fin they come in, I jist stick them ahen the clock.'

'Bit ye must dee something wi them some time.'

'Ay! Fin the clock faas doon.'

THE DAY'S sheepdog trials at Monymusk had gone rather well and the winner, Airchie, was being feted left, right and centre at the wee lounge bar out by the village.

A couple from Winnipeg were on holiday. They were from farming stock and had been most impressed.

'Say Archie, I'll give you a thousand dollars for that dog,' said the Canadian.

Airchie made no comment, but a Welsh enthusiast from the dales was also taken by the dog. 'Well sir, I am a keen triallist myself,' he said, 'and I would love that dog, too, but I'm afraid four hundred pounds is my limit.'

The Canadian upped his bid to three thousand and the impassive Airchie was not swayed until later in the evening when, over a few drams, he decided to take the Welshman's offer.

His erstwhile pal, Geordie, said: 'Ye daft bugger. Ye've refused three thoosan dollars an taen the peerer offer. Ye're aff yer heid.'

Puffing his pipe with an air of contentment, Airchie reasoned:

'Weel, kennin Flossie, gin she gets doon the length o Wales, she'll seen win her wye hame, bit I'm damnt sure she'll nae sweem the Atlantic.'

Characters

They say that characters are the fuel on which any region's humour is based. Some say that the fuel is running dry, which seems a thochtie pessimistic to us. Here is proof that the Doric is all the richer for the legacy of its notables, past and present.

HARRY SIM was one of the most colourful councillors in Aberdeenshire local government, and is sadly missed.

Once, he was a Grampian Regional Council delegate to the Offshore Technology Council in Houston, Texas, where anyone who is anyone in the global oil industry has to make an appearance.

As we all know, where high-spending businesspeople gather, working girls are never far behind, and the OTC attracts 'friendly' women from throughout the southern states.

So it was that George Durward, now of Aberdeen, and Harry found themselves sharing a lift in their Houston hotel with a long-limbed ebony beauty, obviously heading off for an evening's commerce.

Presently, her gaze lighted on Harry. She smiled, leaned across to him and suggested that he might be looking for company for the night.

A devoted family man, Harry was outraged. 'Lassie,' he said, pulling himself up to his full 5 feet, 'awa and dip yer erse in ice cubes.'

THE LEGENDARY Harry Gordon was a national celebrity for his variety shows, comedy sketches and recordings in the Thirties, Forties and Fifties but, outgoing as he was professionally, he liked to keep his private life to himself and was not keen on accepting too many invitations to dinners or parties.

'Are you lonesome the nicht?'

Habitually, when sent an invitation to some function or another, he would reply very courteously:

'Thank you very much for your kind invitation to dinner on Friday next but, unfortunately, I must decline as I cannot be sure that I will be hungry that night.'

THE BUS station at Ballater was in its usual sleepy state one morning in the late 1950s, when Erchie (not his real name; we'll spare him) reported for duty, clocking in at eight, ready to take the wifies in to The Toon on a Saturday-morning shopping spree.

Erchie hadn't many bad habits but, for relaxation, a rug o the pipe stappit wi bogie roll was the very dab.

Inspectors from Bluebird buses (or was it Strachan's at that time?) had the nasty habit of turning up when least expected, and this eagle-eyed official spotted our faithful driver walking into the garage close by the diesel tanks and the No Smoking sign, pipe puffing away like a steam mill.

The inspector followed him in, and here's how a colleague got the first-hand report from our Erchie.

'The peakit-bonnetit mannie challenged me an tellt me I wid be reportit for smokin on duty. Man, I took es cuttie fae ma pooch and I said: "Na, faith ye. Ere's ma pipe and check for yersel. It's steen caul." '

The inspector, although far from impressed, had to admit defeat.

Erchie continued his account: 'Losh, I cwidna get the mannie awa quick eneuch, for the ither pipe wis reid hett and burnin a hole in ma pooch.'

THE LATE Sir Maitland Mackie used to tell a story – he had many – of his farming days at Westerton, Rothienorman.

One of his favourites told of a farmer in earlier days who was always trying to be modern. The usual manure at that time was mixed on the floor of the sheds and then put on to the field. However, the farmer would try the latest on the market – finely ground compounds which the grieve was quite sure could not possibly be any good.

Reluctantly, the grieve had to carry out the boss's wishes and put the men to the work; a happer each, side by side, throwing the stuff out.

Just before lowsin time, the orraman came with the news that there was not sufficient manure to finish out the last wee bit.

The grieve replied: 'Gawa back and tell them ti wug their airms. It'll mak nae bliddy difference.'

GEORGE CLARK, the noted heavy-events athlete on the games scene, took over a hotel at Bonar Bridge and, of course, put out an invitation to his bosom – or boozin – pals to come up North sometime and see his new place.

Three lads, indeed, made the journey once George had settled in, and arrived just on the stroke of 11 – opening time.

After pleasantries had been swapped, the first of the trio said: 'OK, George, we'll hae three drams.'

George reached for the optic and turned back to his pals.

'And which o you three buggers is nae drinkin?'

FOR YEARS, Jimmy Hepburn was manager of the George Walker & Sons fish-selling office at Mallaig, taking over from his father who left Gamrie to start selling for his East Coast firm.

Jimmy didn't suffer fools gladly and it was seldom that anyone got the better of him. A difficult skipper from the East making a rare trip into Mallaig with his catch was not at all happy with the price he was getting, nor the service, and swore that never again would he sell any catch through Jimmy.

'Weel, ma freen,' said Jimmy, his patience at breaking

point. 'I'm fifty-four year aul noo and for fifty-three o them I never kent ye existit. I got on gran athoot ye and I'm sure I'll continue that wye even if I nivver see ye again.'

WILLIE GRAY, the Bard o Briggies, summed up a fellow-Donside countryman rather well with the remark:

'Dammit, he's that lazy he cwidna even be bathert ti shak fin he wis caul.'

WILLIE (not our bard we hasten to add) was a gentle soul who lived by himself at Cullerlie and was the orraman at neighbouring farms. He led a rather spartan existence and his intelligence would have been classed as below average.

Coming to autumn, he would go through his annual ritual of storing the fuel for the fire. Peats and sticks would be taken in to his bothy and built up alongside a wall. Paper would be strewn on the floor and the fire lit with the assistance of a suppie paraffin.

One year, the inevitable happened and a massive fire made poor Willie homeless. He was such a loveable character that in no time the neighbours had clubbed together to get him a caravan to be sited on the shell of the bothy because he couldn't bear to leave the area.

The following autumn, Willie began the same ritual of storing his peats and lighting his fires and, sadly, lightning does strike in the same place twice. Once again, his home was destroyed in a raging blaze. With the walls of the caravan being flimsy, this one was much quicker than the first.

The fire brigade from Alford attended as they had done on the previous occasion, and fireman Jock Milne, one of the most notorious characters in the Howe of Alford, said:

'Michty Willie, mind me ti gie ye a calendar at Christmas. Ye're wir best customer.'

SADLY, IT was decided that Willie had to uproot, and he found a home in a complex at Oldmeldrum for elderly people. It didn't take him long to settle, however, as two friends discovered when they went to visit him. Willie was proud to show them round 'his place'.

'Es is ma bedroom. Es is far I sleeps. Es is the lounge far we aa watch the tee vee and play cairds.'

Then, opening the bathroom door, he said: 'And es is the dipper. They've hid me in twice.'

CHARLIE ROSS, the forester, and Harry, the souter o Dunecht, were great pals – Harry being the father of one of your co-authors.

They had been in Garlogie Bar, a mere four miles from base, when the souter expressed a wee bit of anxiety that 'it wis time they were takkin the road'.

'Michty souter,' said the forester, 'time for anither een.'

That one for the road was doubled and trebled, with the souter getting more and more agitated.

'Lord, Harry,' said our happy forester. 'Tak my advice. If ye're five meenits late, ye get a bugger o a row. If ye're five days late, she's damnt gled tae see ye.'

THE LATE John Mearns, that doyen of couthy country humour, was compèring a concert at the Burns Club in Aberdeen. Among the soloists was his wife, Alice. She was requested to sing the 'Back o Bennachie', and unaccompanied, since no piano was available.

Unfortunately, she started a key higher than was comfortable for her, but she struggled on to the usual applause.

Coming back on stage, John said: 'Weel, Alice, Bennachie's nae affa hich, bit it's been some hich for you the nicht.'

IN THE Thirties and Forties, Nath the Donkey was a well-known figure in the Buckie area as he plied his trade, selling vegetables and bartering household items for rags. This was all done from a small cart drawn by a donkey.

On one of his weekly visits to Findochty, the local worthy had bought her veggies and returned indoors only to hear Nath shouting loud abuse at his donkey. Back out she came and said: 'Guid be here, Nath. Fit's aa the tidee?'

'It's ma donkey,' the merchant replied. 'It winna shift an inch and I've tried aathing.'

Our redoubtable lady had the answer.

'Weel, Nath, jist ee peel een o yer ingins and stick half o't up the donkey's doup.'

This he did and the donkey shot off at great haste leaving Nath on the pavement starin at the vanishin cart.

'Oh me, oh me. Fit wye wull I get him back noo?'

'Weel,' said the wife. 'Try shovin the ither half up yer ain doup.'

IAN MIDDLETON told of Kirsty, a redoubtable figure in Buckie in the Sixties, who was becoming decidedly peeved that a nosy male neighbour was for ever glowering into her window every time he passed her house.

One July, in the middle of a great day of heat, Kirsty had opened her window to let in a blaa of fresh air. The nosy mannie took this as an invitation to have a longer glower, and Kirsty's patience finally snapped.

Throwing up her skirt, she stuck her rump to the window and shouted: 'Can ye nae read sma print?!'

DOD MURRAY was a well-loved Buckie skipper with a great wit and tolerance, but he was fed up with one of his crew, who was telling his mates constantly that his wife was 'an angel'.

'That's gran,' said Dod. 'I'm rale pleased for ye. Mine's aye livin.'

The Toon

The friendly rivalry between city and country, Teuchter and Toonser, is at its best in their sense of humour. Here are a few examples of golden wit from the Silver City.

FRANK TAYLOR was a post-war delivery driver for Paterson's, the wholesale chemist's in Aberdeen, and was a weel-kent figure around the city, with his faithful horse, laden cart and Trixie the dog.

One day, Mitchell Ross, owner of the firm, decided that the march of progress was inevitable and informed Frank that the horse would have to be retired and that he would be issued with a brand-new Commer truck.

Frank was none too happy, but agreed to the change.

After several weeks without his beloved horse, a city chemist asked Jack how he was getting on with the Commer.

'Ach,' said Frank. 'The horse kept awa fae the traffic, but this bugger gyangs stracht for it.'

THE TALES of the country-bred waitress at the old Gloucester Hotel, which we featured in *A Dash o' Doric*, seemed to take a trick, especially with those readers who remembered the doughty lady only too well. Bette Fraser, now living in Dunfermline, remembers being invited out by a boyfriend in the late 1950s and finishing with dinner at the Gloucester.

'I can't be certain that your waitress and mine were the same,' she wrote, 'but her tongue was razor-sharp and she was very entertaining with it. To be perfectly honest, I had grown tired of my young man, for he was a wee bit full of himself and a bit showy-offy, and it was time he was taken down a peg.

'The waitress came to ask if we would like a drink before our meal, and my lad puffed out his chest and said: "Yes, I

think I will have a G and T." Then he laughed in her face
and said: "That's a gin and tonic."

' "Is that so?" she said. "And wid ye like ice and lemon?
That's frozen watter and sliced fruit." '

THE SAME doughty waitress is supposed to have been
stopped by a breakfast guest who wanted to complain that
his egg was off.

She glared at him and said: 'I only biled it. I didna lay it.'

AND STILL in full flight, she is supposed to have served a
cup of coffee to a QC who was having a break from court.
Unfortunately, he had not been given a teaspoon.

He made a grave error in trying sarcasm. 'Waitress,' he
said, 'this coffee is a little too hot to stir with my fingers,
isn't it?'

'Ach weel,' she said, sailing past, 'wait a twa-three
minties and try again.'

SOME YEARS ago, when Brazil were playing Scotland in
a friendly international at Hampden, there was a sizeable
exodus from the North-east eager to lend support to the
boys in blue.

Two of Torry's finest found themselves outside the
national stadium and spotted a dusky-skinned gentleman,
obviously from South America, looking a little lost. They
decided to see if they could help.

'Aye-aye,' said one. 'Ye're lookin lost. Far are ye fae?'

The Brazilian looked mystified.

'Where – are – you – fae?' said the other Aberdonian.

The foreigner brightened. 'Ah. I am from Rio de Janeiro.'

'Rio de Janeiro?' said one of the Torry loons. 'Michty,
fit time did ye leave the hoose?'

EILEEN DUNN started work at the Watt & Grant store
in Union Street shortly before the war and recalls two

The horseless carriage

country wifies leaving after having spent fully three hours raking through frocks and trying on this, that and the other.

Eventually, they left having purchased nothing, but Eileen heard one say to the other as they headed for the door:

'I really likit that green een, Jessie.'

'Ay,' said Jessie, 'it wid hiv fittit ye if ye could hiv got it on.'

TOWARDS THE end of her career, Eileen worked among lingerie and recalls a very shy and embarrassed young man turning up and surveying the goods on sale. Eileen debated whether or not he might want help or if he might find that offputting.

Eventually, she approached him and asked quietly if he needed assistance.

'Ay, w-well,' he stammered. 'I w-wis lookin for a silk nightie or something.'

'Certainly,' said Eileen. 'What size and what colour and I'll show you a few styles?'

A little happier with himself, the young chap looked through the items which Eileen had spread out on the counter and, as he surveyed, he mentioned that it was a birthday present for his wife.

'Oh, lovely,' said Eileen. 'When's her birthday?'

'It's nae her birthday,' he said. 'It's my birthday.'

EILEEN ALSO recalls serving two women who had arrived in the store one Saturday in April. One woman was looking for an outfit for a forthcoming wedding, and her friend was there to give a second opinion.

The customer went through several dresses, each with less success than the one before, until eventually the friend studied the seventh attempt and said: 'Nae really.'

'Nae really?' snapped the customer to her friend. 'Fit div

ye mean nae really? Is it the wrang colour? The wrang style? The wrang linth? Fit is't?'

The friend walked forward and patted her chum on the shoulder. 'Pit it this wye, Ina. Ye look lik a bugfae o cats awa ti be droont.'

SHEILA INNES, of Mannofield, Aberdeen, was sitting having lunch in rather a rundown city-centre café one day listening to the old couple at the next table. The woman was chawing happily at her bradie and chips, but the old boy clearly did not rate the cuisine very highly and grumbled all the way through.

Shortly before Sheila was due to go, a plumber's van arrived outside and the plumber and his mate took various hacksaws, blowlamps, hammers and spanners from the back of the van and marched into the shop.

'Ay boys,' said the old grumbler, looking up. 'I see ye've aeten here afore.'

JIMMY MAUCHRIE was a famous old-style barber in George Street until his early death in 1958. The story goes that a bald gentleman turned up for a trim but, before he sat down, he wanted to know how much he would be charged.

When he found out he would be charged the normal price for a trim, he objected strongly.

'Ye're nae tellin me ye're chargin full price for a haircut and me wi sae little hair?'

'I am,' said Jimmy. 'Cuttin yer hair hardly costs onythin. The pricey bit's findin it.'

POSTIE BARRY had just returned to his base at the Head Post Office in Crown Street, Aberdeen, after his first delivery and told his colleague that he had been stung by a wasp on his rounds.

'Far aboot?' inquired John.

'Osborne Place.'

DOLLY AND Harry Birnie, of Aberdeen, were on holiday in London. On the last day, they were looking for those obligatory last-minute take-home presents.

They couldn't forget their dear friend Alfie back home in the Granite City, an inveterate smoker, so that was why they came to enter a very posh tobacconist's shop in the Bond Street area.

They were shown a wide selection of pipes, but were recommended one meerschaum in particular which was very, very expensive.

Dolly examined the pipe, put it back down on the counter and said to the pukka gentleman at the other side.

'Ach, no. At's ower muckle. He'll jist let it fa, trump on't an brakk it.'

They departed the shop leaving behind a totally bewildered assistant.

A MAJOR fish-processing firm in Poynernook Road, Aberdeen, had just installed the latest in machinery, with filleting and packing lines instead of the conventional tables.

The filleters on the line, upwards of 50 perhaps, were mostly women and it was a new and daunting experience for the young male management to run the gauntlet of the tongues of the fishwives.

In fact, it became too much; the wifies won with their wit every time, so the production manager and his sidekick decided on safety in numbers.

From thenceforth, they would inspect the work in pairs, most distinctive in their white coats, wellies and starched hats.

With such a close relationship, it didn't take the filleting quines long to chorus:

'Here they are again – semmit and draa'ers.'

The Papers

The Press and Journal, Evening Express *and a whole raft of weeklies from Forres to Montrose have recorded thousands of funny Doric stories in their time. Often, the funniest are those which befall the reporters and writers.*

DURING CAMPAIGNING for the 1955 General Election, it was the practice for candidates to tour constituencies making up to three speeches a night at various rural halls. In the days before TV, a good turnout was guaranteed, and so it was at a hall up one Kincardine glen.

Jimmy Lees, then an Aberdeen Journals reporter, reckons that the audience topped 100, made up mostly of farmers, farm-workers and wives, all waiting to hear what the candidate would have to say.

But the candidate was late and the minutes ticked away – 10, 20, then half an hour.

With the audience becoming restless, the MC, a local farmer himself, tried to steady the assembly by calling from the stage: 'A'richt, a'richt, ladies and gentlemen, as ye can see, the candidate's a bittie late, bit I've nae doot he'll be here afore lang. Hooivver, we'll fill in the time wi a discussion, I think. Now, fit will we discuss? His onybody got a suggestion?'

There was silence in the hall.

'Naebody ata?' said the MC. 'A'richt, I'll pick a subject masel.'

He thought for a moment, then brightened.

'I ken,' he said. 'Seein that this rural depopulation's worryin a'body, we'll hae a discussion on that. Now, we ken it's a problem. We'll seen hae nae fowk left up the glens. So, tell me noo, foo wid ye stop rural depopulation?'

'Nae bother,' came a shout from the back. 'Lat louse yer grieve.'

FROM TIME to time, Radio 1 forsakes its London studios and travels around the country. On one occasion in the late 1980s, the station broadcast its entire live output from Aberdeen and, for a whole morning, from the premises of Aberdeen Journals.

A succession of DJs on the morning in question toured the various departments, broadcasting to the nation from the likes of the press room, the editorial hall and the advertising building.

The broadcast from Advertising fell to Bruno Brookes, who decided that he would like to interview an advertising rep and asked for a suitable nominee, but the young woman who was volunteered seemed not at all happy about broadcasting live to millions across the nation. We'll call her Joanne to spare her blushes.

To try to put her at her ease, Bruno said he would give her a little rehearsal while the two-minute news bulletin was being broadcast. Sure enough, when the news began, he explained to Joanne that he would ask her an easy-enough question about the cost of advertising in regional papers these days, and wasn't it horrendously expensive. 'What will your reply be?' he asked.

Joanne was prompted by her colleagues to point out that, for the money, advertisers were getting unparalleled access to virtually half the adult population of the North of Scotland so that the per-head fee was one of the lowest of any form of advertising. Not only that, but newspaper advertising's track record in shifting goods for sale remained unmatched.

Joanne felt happy with that, but looked anxiously at the microphone in front of her and at the location manager counting down the seconds until the broadcast went live to the nation once more. A light sweat appeared on her brow.

Once the news had finished and the red light had illuminated in front of Bruno Brookes, he began in his customarily bouncy style:

Politicians in a spin

'Welcome back to Aberdeen, where we're broadcasting across the nation from one of Scotland's leading newspaper companies. With me is Joanne, who sells advertising for two of the most successful newspapers in the country. Now, tell me, Joanne, people say to me that it's all very well advertising in newspapers, but it's very expensive. Now, tell me honestly, as the expert you are, the cost is really horrific, isn't it?'

Joanne swallowed hard, began sweating profusely, looked at the mike and said:

'Ay.'

DOUG PRATT, a reporter from the *Press and Journal*, had been sent out to meet a centenarian in a Church of Scotland eventide home in Aberdeen and had been surprised and delighted to find a sparky, elegant and lively woman who looked at least 20 years younger, with hair newly done, a little make-up, new frock and clearly enjoying being the centre of attention.

'Tell me,' said Doug, 'why do you suppose you've been able to live to be a hundred?'

She leaned forward and tapped his knee mischievously.

'The good Lord enjoys lettin me annoy ivry ither bugger in here.'

WHEN 'MAD' Colin Mitchell was campaigning as Tory candidate for West Aberdeenshire in 1970, he attended a lively meeting at Inverurie Town Hall. Mad Mitch was lamenting the fact that unemployment seemed to be increasing under the Labour government and that many more people were on short-term working contracts. He spotted one dejected looking soul in the second row and asked him:

'You, sir. Are you in work?'

The man nodded.

'And what time do you go to work?'

The man removed his bunnet, scratched his head and sighed: 'I'm a fairmer. I dinna ging ti work. Ilky mornin I wakken up, I'm surroundit wi the bliddy stuff.'

THE HIGHLAND Games scene in Grampian area has its climax at the famed Braemar Gathering in the Princess Royal and Duke of Fife Memorial Park. The attendance of members of the Royal Family as they holiday at Balmoral swells the crowd to around 20,000, but it extends the resources of the security forces and puts pressure on the committee who put on the gathering.

Perhaps it's his rustic Deeside upbringing, but organising secretary Bill Meston takes each problem as it comes and one came early one year in the form of a persistent Pressman who was anxious to speak to Bill as secretary, even although his channel of communication should have been the Press tent.

He had already had two abortive sorties into the small secretary's tent to be told that Bill was out on the field somewhere.

On his third visit he tried again, and there he was face-to-face with Bill, whom he didn't know.

'Is Mr Meston around *now*?' enquired our anxious hack-cum-photographer.

Rather than explain the whole rigmarole of the procedures to be adhered to through the two officials in charge of the Press tent, the reply from Bill was short but effective.

'Losh, he canna be far awa; I've been wi him aa mornin.'

IT'S GOING back a wee bit, but it shows that your authors have the North-east at heart.

It's so long ago that your co-author cannot recall the date when Alastair Robertson wrote a column in the *Evening Express* – Bon-Accord Gossip – and it featured a dilemma facing Robbie.

There had come an invitation for him to compère the Scottish Fiddle Orchestra, conducted by the redoubtable John Mason MBE – at the Royal Albert Hall in London.

Unfortunately, it coincided with Meldrum Sports and our commentator politely refused the London invitation. This prompted Mr Robertson to write:

'Robbie Shepherd forsakes glamour of city lights of London to commentate on egg-and-spoon race at Meldrum.'

SPOTTED IN one weekly paper's report from the small courts:

'A woman has been charged with growing cannabis at Huntly Sheriff Court.'

Michty, fit's the law comin til?

THE *Press and Journal* has a network of what are known in the trade as corrs, short for correspondents. These are people in towns, villages and parishes throughout the paper's circulation area – the northern half of Scotland – who are of good character and who can keep an ear to the ground for likely stories.

Some of the more accomplished are trusted almost as professional reporters and the newsdesk relies on them to do a near-professional job, which is why, in the 1964 election, it was a corr who was assigned to cover the count of one North-east constituency, mainly because the result was judged to be a walkover for the sitting member, and there was not likely to be anything untoward to demand the efforts of a professional newsman.

Unfortunately, as well as taking details of the count, the corr had partaken a little too heavily of the hospitality. Back in Aberdeen, the newsdesk staff were becoming more and more anxious that what should have been a straight-forward phone-in seemed to be getting perilously close to edition time.

Eventually, the corr phoned.

'And the reshult here,' he slurred, '. . . is . . . is . . . and the reshult . . . the reshult . . . the v-v-vohhhhhhte . . . the reshult . . . is . . . is. Michty, I'm an affa mess o drink.'

It was the one time the *Press and Journal* missed an election result on its own doorstep, through no fault of its own.

Aches and Pains

The doctor has an unrivalled perspective for seeing North-east wit at its most vulnerable, and some of the best stories come when the inhibitions are down and the semmits are up.

DR PAT Macdonald, who was in general practice in Aberdeen before retiring to Beaconsfield in the Home Counties of England, told of examining an elderly lady who was very concerned about her health, but who couldn't quite state what she thought was wrong with her or what her symptoms were.

Pat called in the nurse and began the examination, and kept up light-hearted chatter through his questioning, but still could find nothing wrong.

'Well,' he said, sitting back at his desk, 'you'll be pleased to hear that you're as well as can be expected Miss ——. You'll live to be eighty, at least.'

He was horrified when the woman said: 'Bit I am eichty.'

But he said he could have hugged his country-born nurse when, quick as a flash, she stepped in with: 'Weel, so the doctor's richt again.'

OVERHEARD IN the dentist's waiting-room at the Bridge of Don. An elderly lady and her daughter were waiting, and granny, as we'll call her, was to be fitted for a new set of false teeth.

'Weel,' said the daughter, 'I jist hope ye dinna end up lookin lik Esther Rantzen.'

A puzzled look came over granny's face.

'Fa's he?'

IN *A Dash o' Doric*, we told the true story of a patient at Aberdeen Royal Infirmary and the aftermath of his operation.

To recap: Willie woke up to find the curtains drawn round about him and a nurse standing there with a basin of hot water, a bar of soap and a towel.

'Now, Willie, ye're gettin a bed-bath.'

'Michty, nursie,' said Willie. 'Ye'll nivver get my erse in that sma basin.'

Now to the other side of the North-easter, and it's in response to that story that we heard from Mrs Sim, of Stoneywood, who had a similar tale but with a different ending.

Sandy was a retiring bachelor in his seventies in similar circumstances to Willie – the curtains, the soap, the basin, and so on.

'Richt Sandy. Ye're gettin on fine noo, so we're gaun tae gie ye a bed-bath.'

But Sandy had never tirred in front of a female before and, after much stuttering and stammering, he said grudgingly:

'Aa richt than, bit jist leave the roch grun ti me.'

A PATIENT at Aberdeen Royal Infirmary was undergoing a stomach operation under a local anaesthetic and was asked by the surgeon if he was feeling all right.

'Aye. I'm aa richt,' said the patient, 'bit I'm maist damnable thirsty. I cwid dee fine wi a drink o waater.'

'Weel,' said our surgeon of the North-east, responding in the patient's vernacular, 'If ye can jist hing on a meenitie. Ye see, ivnoo we've got nae wye ti pit it.'

IAN MIDDLETON, of Arradoul, near Buckie, recalled a spell in hospital at Aberdeen Royal Infirmary. Lying in the next bed was Wullie, from Strichen, who had fractured his hip.

To keep any unnecessary weight off his legs, a cage was put over them with the downie on top. Coming out of the anaesthetic, he was extremely raivelt and Ian had to call for the nurse when Wullie started to crank his legs at an alarming rate.

'What's the matter, Wullie?' asked the nurse.

'I canna get tae Strichen,' said Wullie. 'There's nae pedals in this bugger o a thing.'

WHEN YOUR co-author who works for the daily paper was visiting his mother during a rare spell in hospital, he found himself intrigued by the occupant of the next bed, an elderly lady from one of the tiny fisher villages between Fraserburgh and Peterhead.

We'll call her Elsie to protect her identity, but she was an absolute charmer.

'Fit div ye think I'm in for?' she asked him one evening.

He shrugged his shoulders.

'Weel, it's nae that,' she said, pointing at the cage over her lower legs. 'That's twa broken legs, that.'

'But you say you're not in for those,' he said.

'No,' she said. 'That broken legs happened in the operatin theeter. I went doon and ma legs wis a'richt. I come back and they wis baith broken. I'm sure they drappit me aff the table.'

'That's terrible.'

'Of coorse it's terrible. And me in the hospital, tee. Ye dinna expect ti get yer legs broke in a hospital, div ye? Nae baith o them, onywye. Waur nor that, I gied doon ti get ma appendix oot and fin I come back and the gas wore aff there's a notie waitin for me fae the surgeon sayin that they'd found something else in ma intimmers fin they wis pokin aboot, but seein as I hidna gien ma consint for onything abeen ma appendix, they couldna dee nithing aboot it til I signed on the dottit line. So they jist shooed me back up and sent me a notie. Hiv ye ivver heard the like? I mean, they wis pokin aboot inside me fitivver; I widna hiv mindit gettin the hale jing-bang deen a' at the same time.

'So here I am, back up in this bed wi twa broken legs, recovering fae gettin ma appendix wheepit oot and noo I'm waitin for anither operation that I didna even ken I needit.'

She sank back on her pillows, exhausted with the exertions of her story.

Then she looked up again: 'I wis near a'richt fin I come in here,' she said. 'I'll be gaun hame a bliddy wreck.'

A FEW misunderstandings from the files of patients' reports, as told to us by a receptionist at Aberdeen Royal Infirmary. Transcribing from the dictaphone to typewritten words can be tricky sometimes.

'The patient was admitted for high thigh amputation.'
appeared as
'The patient came in for Hi-Fi amputation.'

'Cystoscope passed easily.'
was translated as
'Sister Cope passed easily.'

'The abdomen was opened and there was pus.'
appeared as
'The abdomen was opened and there was puss.'

'Her mouth, tongue and fauces were healthy.'
became
'Her mouth, tongue and falsies were healthy.'

Law and Order

Beneath the grave exterior of the due process of law, a healthy sense of humour is alive and well. Best of all, it's often directed inwards.

YOU CAN'T help feeling sorry for Abbie Innes, of Aberdeen, who drove to Glasgow for the first time in 1989 and admits that he must have been travelling just a shade over the speed limit when a flashing blue light appeared in his rear-view mirror.

He pulled over to the side and waited for the traffic officer to appear at his window. The officer duly appeared and invited Abbie for a discussion in the back seat of the patrol car.

Facing incredible odds, our North-east man decided to lay on the Doric as broadly as he could, hoping to touch the bobby's heart with the plight of an obvious country bumpkin bewildered in the big city.

'I didna ken fit yer signs meant, ye see,' he said, adding by way of explanation: 'I'm fae Aiberdeen.'

'Well, sir,' said the bobby, 'funnily enough, the signs mean the same doon here as they mean in Aberdeen.'

JIMMY IRVINE, who retired to a croft near Banff, recalls his days as a travelling salesman and being stopped for speeding between Inverurie and Huntly.

The traffic officer read him the charge and asked if he had anything to say. Jimmy thought it might help his case if he explained how many miles he travelled, in perfect safety, every year.

'Ye ken this,' he said, 'I've driven a' ower the country since 1953, maybe thirty – forty-thoosan mile a year, and this is the first time I've been stoppit.'

The bobby looked decidedly underwhelmed.

'In that case,' he said, 'we should hiv stoppit ye a lang time ago.'

A HARASSED mother arrived at Lumsden police station to complain about her own son, who was getting more than a little out of hand.

'He jist winna dee fit he's tell't,' she said.

She asked the bobby if he would maybe turn up at their house some night and speak to the young rascal in the hope that that might give him 'a dasht good scare'.

'Eer face is as ugly's mine,' said our country constable. 'Awa hame and scare him yersel.'

JIMMY WAS the old-style bobby nearing the end of his service to the community in the old Moray and Nairn Constabulary. He maybe wasn't among the ranks of the new liberated thinkers, but his philosophy was that you couldn't teach old dogs or cops new tricks.

He had risen through the ranks to Inspector with his honest-to-goodness approach and might well have been the originator of the E for Aeple callsign we highlighted in *A Dash o' Doric*.

The patrol car with Inspector Jimmy (we hide his real identity) and Constable John was on Harbour Street, Nairn, when Jimmy thought it was time to report in.

'Car twenty-seven to Echo. Am patrolling north on Harbour Street, Nairn, and approaching the harbour.'

Back came an unidentified voice to an unamused inspector:

'Haud gyan.'

FROM THE same branch of Her Majesty's Constabulary, we heard of the superintendent who applied for a more senior post, listing among his qualifications that he had been dux of his school. One of his fellow-supers was heard to remark:

'Dux at his skweel? Goad Almichty: sivven pupils.'

Ken your road signs

IT WAS maybe this rival superintendent who was the main player in this next story.

Sandy was an extremely able policeman and came of a very old, established farming family. With his service years about up, he couldn't wait to get his police pension and head back to the family farm.

We speak of the days when all photography was done by the CID, including taking pictures at fatal road accidents. The photographs were then approved by the duty superintendent before being passed over to the fiscal.

On this occasion, a detective-sergeant went up with a batch of photographs of wreckage and general mayhem, some of which was on the roadway and some in an adjoining turnip field.

The superintendent studied the prints, going back to one general view several times. Eventually he gave his verdict. Handing this print back to the sergeant, he said:

'Man, isn't that a gran level park o neeps?'

WE ARE indebted to John Duff, that former policeman and stalwart of the Braemar Mountain Rescue Team, for this one and a few more on the subject of bobbies.

Former Chief Inspector Peter MacInnes came straight from his native Skye to be the first recruit to the Scottish Northeastern Counties Constabulary when it was formed in 1949.

All recruits were stationed at headquarters at Banff until they were allocated to a station. During this waiting period, Peter heard some bloodcurdling stories about the poor bobby who had been posted to Foggieloan.

In due course, Peter learned that he was to be stationed at Aberchirder, and he turned to his neighbour and expressed his heartfelt relief that he had managed to avoid that terrible Foggieloan place.

THE LATE Tom Chasser was Chief Constable of the County of Aberdeenshire from the late Fifties and was a great supporter of the tradition and heritage of the area.

Lonach Gathering took pride of place as far as Highland gatherings were concerned and, as a most gifted after-dinner speaker, he was invited as the main guest at a Lonach Dinner.

In proposing the main toast, he bemused the loyal Men o Lonach by stating that he hadn't realised that the Gaelic tongue was still alive in the strath. Actually, the last native-born Gaelic speaker from those parts had died a good few years previously, but Tom went on to explain his remarks.

Approaching Strathdon with time to spare, he had asked his driver to call in past the Glenkindie Hotel. It was a terrible night of rain and, as he had entered the front door, he had encountered a lad soaked to the skin, parking his cycle by the side of the porch.

They exchanged greetings and, approaching the bar, our Chief Constable was compelled to ask the barman if, indeed, Gaelic was still spoken.

'Oh, there's naebody spikks the Gaelic here,' responded the man behind the counter, to which Tom replied:

'That's strange; when I spoke to that lad at the door he said: "Hooer anicht."'

THE OLD Banffshire Force seemed to produce more characters than the others, possibly because of the number of stills – official and illicit – in the area.

One such bobby was Jimmy Mackie, stationed latterly at Ballindalloch. He and John 'Black Jock' Mowat had joined together in the early Thirties.

Jimmy was to remain unpromoted, although not for lack of native guile, while John rose to become a superintendent and later Deputy Chief Constable.

In the course of his duties as the Deputy Chief, John had occasion to visit Ballindalloch, arriving just as Jimmy had the beets slackened, feet up and was having his post-lunch snooze.

Answering the office doorbell while pulling on his tunic, and not that pleased with the interruption, he saw who his caller was.

He glowered at the DCC.

'Weel,' he barked. 'Are ye Superintendent Mowat the day or are ye jist Jock?'

WE THANK John Duff again for this one showing how quick wit and a certain amount of low cunning can come in handy in the police force.

An Aberlour PC was not found wanting one Games day when, in the course of duty (what else?), he had taken maybe one or two drams too many.

He was seen by a senior officer feeling his way round the rope at the edge of the arena, trying to steady himself. Summoned to account for his actions, he replied:

'Sir, I wis jist feelin the rope in case some o yon young buggers o loons hid cut it.'

TOM CHASSER also told the following story against himself which he swore was true. It might just have been, and it happened soon after his arrival as Chief Constable in the North-east.

Visiting a function one night out of uniform in one of the larger burghs in the force area, he decided to go for a quick stroll and soon came on a bobby in a shop doorway having a quick draw on a fag.

Standing in beside the bobby, he made conversation, realising that he had not been recognised. After a few moments he introduced himself as the Chief Constable, but was totally unprepared for the reply.

Unimpressed, his shop-front companion said:

'Weel, ye've got yersel a damnt fine job.'

THE LATE Willie Merrilees was Lothian Chief Constable in the 1950s and was a great fisherman who liked to venture out on the Spey whenever he found himself with a little spare time. One year, his usual hotel at Grantown was fully booked, so he checked into a smaller, but very comfortable, hotel with its own bar.

As a resident, he could drink there all day and all night if he wanted, but he noticed after a few days that the bar was doing a lively trade among people he suspected were Grantown folk. The locals were dropping in without question.

Purely in a spirit of inquiry, Willie happened to ask the landlord: 'What time do you usually close the bar here?'

'It depends on the fishin,' said the landlord, 'bit usually aboot the end o October.'

Please, Miss

In the front line of Doric humour are the massed ranks of teachers. Judging from our mailbag, there is not a school anywhere in the North-east, primary or secondary, that can't recall the occasional shaft of juvenile wit from some time in its past.

BILL SHAND, now living in the Highlands, retired as an English teacher at a large North-east comprehensive in 1992 and took with him 40 years of memories, particularly of exam-paper blunders. Four of his favourites were:
What caused the Depression?
Lots of people being depressed because they hadn't any money.
and
What is the correct name for your father's father?
George.
and
When we say an animal is sure-footed, what does that mean?
Every time it kicks you, it never misses.
and
Define the term 'circle'.
A circle is a round line with no kinks or corners, joined up again so that you can't tell where it started.

AND FROM Banff Academy:
Ferdinand Magellan circumcised the world with a 200ft clipper.

AND IN the mid-1970s a terse telephone call from an angry parent reached Inverurie Academy. The man was outraged that his offspring's illness should be queried by a suspicious teacher, who had demanded further information:

'Foo div ye spell blunder?'

'Foo wid I ken fit's wrang with ma loon?' he demanded. 'And foo wid I ken fan he'll be back? I'm nae Houdini.'

VIOLET THOMSON was a primary teacher at a rural Buchan school in the mid-1960s and had decided to teach a lesson on weather. After discussing rain, snow and sunshine, she moved on to the topic of thunder and lightning. She asked for someone to explain how they thought thunder and lightning happened.

There was a long silence until eight-year-old Victor, whose domain was his father's farm, shot up a brosey arm.

'Yes, Victor?'

'Please, Miss,' drawled Victor, 'ma mither says it's the Baby Jesus playin wi the licht switch and God giein him a skelpit erse.'

MISS THOMSON also recalls teaching a class of eight-year-olds at a school in rural Strathbogie in the late 1950s when the subject for the afternoon was mental arithmetic. Willie was not a particularly quick thinker at the best of times, but when asked to add nine and seven he was thoroughly stumped.

'Is it eichteen, miss?' he asked.

'Now, now, Willie,' she said gently. 'You're just guessing.'

'Sivventeen?'

'Enough of that, now. You know perfectly well nine and seven are sixteen.'

Miss Thomson said she was about to move on to the next sum, but had to turn to the blackboard to stifle a smile when, out of the corner of her eye, she saw Willie lean to the boy next to him and whisper: 'What a bliddy caper. She said *eicht* and *eicht* wis sixteen.'

TO KEITH Grammar School, where a first-year pupil was struggling badly with a problem of geometry. No matter how hard he tried, Sandy couldn't make head nor tail of the odd-looking shape on the paper in front of him.

'Come on, Sandy,' said his teacher. 'You know how to work out the area of odd-looking shapes. You break down the shape into littler shapes that are easier to work out, like squares and triangles, and then you add it all up and you've got the total area.'

Sandy scratched his head and looked as blank as ever.

'All right,' said his teacher, trying a new tack. 'You're a farmer's son.'

Sandy's chest puffed out. 'Ay,' he said proudly.

'All right, so imagine this shape is one of your father's parks. If you draw a line here . . . and here . . . you're left with a rectangle, a long thin triangle on one side and a short fat triangle on the other.'

Sandy looked as if the fog might be clearing.

'So work out the sizes of the rectangle and the two triangles for me and you've got the area of the park.'

Sandy set about the task with renewed vigour. After five minutes he shouted the teacher back and showed her his answer. It was correct and he beamed with pride, then added: 'Bit what a helluva aakward park ti ploo.'

A CHEMISTRY class at Turriff Academy in the mid-1960s was discussing the metal-eating properties of acid. The teacher had dropped a succession of small bits of metal into a beaker of sulphuric acid and the class had watched the metals fizz and dissolve, or burst into flames, or sputter round the surface before disappearing.

Finally, the teacher fumbled in his pocket and pulled out a half-crown.

'Now,' he said, 'here's a half-crown. I'm going to drop it into the acid. Will it dissolve?'

There was a short silence while the class considered the proposal, then Leslie put up his hand.

'Yes, Leslie?'

'No, sir, it winna.'

'And can you explain to the rest of the class why not?'

'Because if it wid, ye widna drap it in the acid.'

OUR SAME source told us of a history class when he was a student teacher at Aberdeen Grammar School. They were discussing the line of succession to the English royal family and had reached Edward VI.

'All right,' he said. 'Queen Mary followed Edward VI, but who followed Mary?'

There was a lot of deep thinking, but a wag at the back of class said: 'Her little lamb.'

WE'VE TO thank Lorna Alexander, of Glenkindie, for this tale of rural schooling in Upper Donside. When Lorna was teaching at Strathdon School, there was a nasty bug on the go and she was feeling decidedly ropey herself.

After returning from the latest of many dashes to the toilet to be sick, a wee lad (one of a big family) put his arms round about her and said soothingly:

'Nivver mind, teacher. Gwa and hae a lie-doon a filie. My mam wis sick es mornin, tee. Dad says it'll be anither bliddy bairn.

'He disna ken foo she manages it.'

THE FRENCH teacher at one prominent North-east grammar school was not having a good day and the class was not responding to her efforts to translate to French.

It was a basic first-week or second-week lesson.

'When I say: "Bonjour, mes enfants," I want your response: "Bonjour, Mademoiselle."'

This was done parrot-fashion in unison, but to find if the message had got through, Mademoiselle decided to try the individual pupils.

She was pleased to see that the teaching appeared to have had its effect – until she came to little Paul.

'Bonjour, mon enfant.'
'Bonjour Madame-yersel.'

PETER SLATER, of Brechin, tells of his wife's cousin, Betty Craig, who was headmistress at Rhynie. She was teaching the young bairns the poem of 'Young Lochinvar' and reached the line: 'Boatman do not tarry.'

Miss Craig paused and asked: 'What does "tarry" mean?'
James shot his hand up.
'Please miss, I ken. It means "dinna scutter".'

Good for the Soul

Between tending to the spiritual needs of their North-east flocks, men (and women) of the cloth have had the odd moment to jot down a few of the more lightsome encounters of their careers. Evidently, dog-collar and wicked sense of humour are not mutually exclusive.

KATHIE ROSS, of Fraserburgh, wrote to say that in the mid-1950s her English spinster aunt had spent a summer on their family farm near Lonmay. One morning, they had spotted the minister. Kathie's aunt had insisted on crossing the road to thank him for a light-hearted and thought-provoking sermon the previous Sunday.

In turn, he thanked her profusely and they chatted for a few minutes more.

'What really surprised me,' said Kathie's aunt, 'was the number of men in the congregation who went straight to the pub afterwards.'

'Ah, yes,' smiled the minister, 'the thirst after righteousness.'

THE REVEREREND Gordon Smith, now retired to Aberdeen, was newly inducted to his Banffshire charge in the late 1940s and had been doing the rounds of his flock. As a single man at the time, he was usually invited to stay for his tea, an offer he accepted every time because the standard of rural fare was invariably excellent.

At one humble village home, he sat down with the family to a sumptuous repast, which was consumed in customary North-east silence.

After the last cup of tea, Mr Smith turned to the woman of the house and complimented her on her cooking. 'It's not often that I have a meal as wonderful as that,' he assured her.

Tending to spiritual needs

The ten-year-old daughter looked at him and sighed: 'Neether div we.'

ETHEL BAIRD, of Kincorth, Aberdeen, was a Sunday School teacher at Stonehaven in the early 1960s and had been teaching a lesson about love and families. The assembly listened attentively – all apart from Arthur, aged eight, who was having none of it.

'I hate ma sister,' he informed Ethel vehemently. 'She's coorse.'

Ethel saw her chance. 'But you don't really mean that, Arthur,' she told him. 'You're maybe angry with her now and again but, mercy, all brothers and sisters have times like that. And always remember that God loves everybody.'

But Arthur remained determinedly unconvinced.

To break the logjam, Ethel suggested that all the class sit quietly and write a letter to God about someone in their families. That night, as she read through them, she came upon Arthur's letter. It began:

'Dear God, I no you love everbody, but yo've never met my sister.'

ETHEL ALSO recalls her cousin's family travelling from Stonehaven to Norfolk to attend the wedding of their son to a young Englishwoman. Also in the party was the groom's five-year-old sister.

When the choirboys entered in their flowing white robes, a five-year-old North-east voice filled the cathedral:

'Look, mam. They're a' gaun ti get a haircut.'

ACCORDING TO the Rev. Charles Birnie, of Strichen, young Jeannie from a small croft up New Aberdour way was in an inquisitive mood, having been told of a distant family death.

'Mam, fin I ging ti Hivven, will Flossie get there as weel?'

'Oh aye, Jeannie; Flossie's a kindly doggie and she'll get there a' richt.'

'An fit aboot Tiddles?'

'Oh aye, I'm sure yer wee cattie'll jine ye tee.'

'And Daisy the coo?'

'Oh weel, I'm nae sae sure there, dearie. Daisy's a muckle beast and there michtna be room for her in Hivven.'

A moment's hesitation, a puzzled look and Jeannie replied: 'Weel, fa's gyan tae hell for the milk?'

RETIRED TEACHER Lilianne Grant Rich has happy memories of childhood, but recalls a little puzzlement at Sunday School.

'I eest tae winner sair,' she recalled, 'fit wye the Gweed Lord preferred tae cut his walkin stick fae the rodden tree in preference tae ony ither trees roon aboot.

'I thocht that the bittie in the twinty-third psalm read: *Thy rodden staff me comfort still.*'

SOME TIME in the Fifties, Pittodrie was booked for an evangelistic experience on a massive scale, with the appearance of America's disciple of God, Billy Graham.

The stadium was packed and, as at the usual football matches, refreshments of the soft nature were available at the start and at half-time.

A special busload attended from Culter, and Eileen McHardy recalled how she found it a most moving experience.

On the way home in the bus, she was contemplating the spiritual uplift of Billy Graham's message and the memorable singing of the choir, and the glory of God and how profound and soul-shaking an evening it had turned out to be, when she heard a rural wifie ask of her companion in the seat behind:

'Wis your pie affa satty?'

IN THE fishing villages of Inverallochy and Cairnbulg, the highlights of the year were the annual Temperance Walks, held on Christmas Day and New Year's Day. Homes were open to anyone who called, and they were invited to partake of the best of food and company. The days ended with the Walk Social, at which the best of the villages' amateur talent would play the flute, recite or sing the old gospel songs.

The village clergy would be there to have their say, and a chairman appointed by the walks committee would lead the evenings' entertainments.

One of the best known chairmen was Eddie Joe's Jockie (a name identifying him by his forebears). At one particular social, Jockie asked his committee in the back room: 'Is a' the meenisters awa?'

'Aye.'

'Gran. We'll awa and tell lees.'

A STORY that predates the National Health Service came from the files of Professor Donald Francis Tovey, of Edinburgh. In the 1930s, the professor told often of the old minister on the Banffshire coast who would thunder and roar at his flock that every one of them would be sure to end in an eternal pit of damnation, a bottomless pit, where every last one of them would spend for ever weeping, wailing and gnashing their teeth.

Then he would pause, look round his congregation, see that most were elderly people and add:

'And for those of you without teeth, teeth will be provided.'

Mony a Gweed Tune

Yet again, one of the most fruitful sources of Doric humour has been the older generation. With far more years to call on, their reminiscences and stories are more varied, more numerous and often the most entertaining. It made it even more difficult for us to decide what to leave out.

GREAT-GRANDMA peered into the week-old bundle of humanity that had been pressed into her bosie. His little hand grasped her crannie and she allowed herself a wee smile. Then she frowned and looked up.

'And fit are ye ca'in him?' she demanded.

'Nathan,' said the proud young mum.

'Awa ye go,' she snapped. 'Ye'll hae ti ca him something.'

OLDER DRIVERS have to take a great deal of criticism for allegedly slow reaction times, which brings us to a tale supplied by a Mr Grant, who lives near Grantown-on-Spey, and was a passenger in a car near Inverurie in 1991 when they had to slow down behind a D-registered saloon being driven by an elderly gentleman.

As they approached a T-junction, where the road widened out into two lanes, the elderly chap switched on his left indicator, so Mr Grant's driver headed for the right-hand lane to turn right. At the same time, the old boy lurched into the right-hand lane, forcing Mr Grant's driver to squeal to an inelegant halt, horn blaring.

The old boy turned right and tootled on, oblivious to the havoc he had caused. Mr Grant's driver decided to tail him to point out his mistake and, a few miles farther on, drew up in front of him and walked back.

'You nearly caused an accident back there,' he stormed. 'Why did you signal left and turn right?'

The old boy, mystified by all the fuss, explained with perfect logic: 'Because ma right flasher's broken.'

Driving everyone round the bend

LOGIC ALSO featured strongly in the report sent to us from Torphins, of an overheard exchange between two elderly women standing at a bus stop in the village one day in July, 1996. Stagecoach evidently wasn't fulfilling their idea of good service, judging by the tone of their conversation.

'This bus service his jist got worse and worse,' said one to the other. 'There's hardly ony buses and they're aye late.'

'Dinna fash yersel,' soothed the other one. 'It'll sort itsel oot afore lang. If Stewartie Milne keeps biggin as mony hooses as he's deein, a' the toons'll seen be oot in the country and we'll hae nae need o buses.'

A PROMINENT landowner and member of the aristocracy whose domain covered large tracts of the North and North-east guarded his privacy zealously, to the extent of enquiring rather brusquely after the business of anyone he found walking on his land.

Early in 1995, he was out for a stroll when he encountered an elderly woman with two small children sauntering up the drive to the big house.

'And what do you think you're doing here, madam?' enquired His Lordship.

'This is ma grandchildren, yer lordship, and I'm takkin them up til the grass in front o the big hoose for a picnic.'

'Indeed, you are not. You can just turn round and have your picnic somewhere else on ground that belongs to you.'

Her gaze narrowed into one of those determined Northeast glowers. 'Ye dinna mind on me, div ye, yer lordship?'

'Should I?'

'Maybe no. Bit mony's the time, fin yer mither wisna aboot, that I gied ye yer bath and changed yer hippens and dichtit yer erse.'

And she sailed on.

SANDY MATHESON was a coach driver in 1973 when he was scheduled to take a party of OAPs from throughout the North-east on a tour to the Italian lakes. He reported standing beside his bus outside the Cowdray Hall, Aberdeen, welcoming his charges as they arrived to begin their off-season adventure.

One of his passengers was a little old lady who had been ferried to the departure point by a little old man, presumably her husband, in a little old Ford Anglia.

'They appeared with enough luggage for half a dozen folk,' wrote Sandy. 'Last of all came a 14-inch portable TV.'

Sandy stopped them as her husband hobbled up the side of the bus looking for somewhere to stow the TV. 'Excuse me,' said Sandy, 'can I ask fit wye ye're takkin a TV on holiday?'

'I canna miss *Crossroads*,' said the woman.

'Bit they dinna hae *Crossroads* on Italian TV,' said Sandy.

'I ken fine,' she snapped, 'and that's fit wye I'm takkin ma ain TV.'

ELMA MASSIE, now of Aberdeen, tells of two old bodies at a North-east WRI meeting discussing the son of a fellow-member. In the old ladies' opinion, the son was affecting a few airs and graces now that he was a successful businessman in London, and had seemed to forget that he came from good, honest North-east stock.

'Ay,' said one to the other. 'He tries ti spik affa weel-dressed.'

WRITER AND fishing historian Peter Buchan used to tell of leading a party of English tourists round the Fish Market and harbour at Peterhead as a favour to a town councillor.

They seemed to show great interest but, at the end, when

Peter asked for questions, one rather clipped lady asked what language it was that people seemed to be speaking to each other.

'That'll be the Doric,' said Peter. 'That's the language we spik up here.'

'It's very strange,' said the woman, looking for a few laughs of approval from her compatriots.

'We manage awa,' said Peter.

'In fact,' said the woman, 'there seem to be an awful lot of strange people up here, full stop.'

'Dinna worry aboot it,' said Peter. 'Maist o' them ging awa hame at the end o the summer.'

THE SCENE is Port Elphinstone, near Inverurie, and the Rev. Douglas Lister's Bible class from St Andrew's Church has visited Blythewood Old Folk's Home to attend a service.

Janice Cottier, an Inverurie quine now in exile in the Isle of Man, recalls the weather being baking hot, but the heating in the home being at full blast, for some reason.

'It was uncomfortably hot,' she wrote, 'but this didn't deter a group of ladies from sitting round a blazing fire.'

'I was talking to an old chap who studied the women and then said to me: "See 'at wifies sittin ower there roon the fire. Fin they get ti Hell, they'll nivver ken the difference."'

BACK TO Alford, and another story of Bessie and Maggie. This is the tale which sticks in everyone's mind in the howe. It involves one of the village plumbers, called to the croft to attend a sink blockage or some such.

He picked his way through two dozen glowering cats and clocking hens and had to dismantle part of the cupboard enclosing the sink to gain access to the piping.

As he pulled off the back panel, the faintly ripe odour he had noticed became thick and sickening.

Out flopped a dead cat.

From the look of her, pussy had been there for several months. The plumber crouched, stammygastered, for a few moments, before he reached in, took the cat's remains by the tail and stood up.

Maggie was watching intently. The plumber turned and wordlessly showed her what he had found. She peered up and down at the lifeless form for a few moments, as if unsure what it was, then her face lit up.

'Gweed sakes,' she said. 'I thocht I'd lost that.'

THE WORD 'homogenised' has crept into the vocabulary with mass sales of milk from major companies supplying to superstore, village shop and doorstep.

Without going into the pros and cons of the modern way of processing, we are reminded of the lady who didn't like the change of a milkman in her street.

The ever-so-friendly Fred with a whistle aye on the lips would bring the pinta right up to her door and Mrs McIntosh was disappointed when he retired.

Such are the pressures of modern deliveries that the new milkie would leave the bottles at the old lady's gate, forcing her to make the few yards in her nightie to pick up the milk before she could have her morning cuppa.

Not too pleased on frosty mornings, she challenged the new lad and dared to suggest that she would even give him an extra penny if he would take the milk right up to the door.

'Weel,' said the fastest milkman in the West. 'If at's the wye ye wint it, jist gie's an extra tippence and I'll tak the coo here itsel the morn and skyte the stuff throwe yer letterbox.'

NOW TO a couple who fancied a new car on their retirement. The husband had been used to driving council lorries all his life, with his elevated seat in the cab looking down on the car drivers below.

His wife insisted that they would not buy anything too big. After all, it was just the two of them, and 'a nice wee car'll dee's fine, John'.

The wee Austin was bought and, after a week, John met up with his pals in the local.

'Foo's retirement, John? And foo's the new Austin?'

'Och, retirement's aa richt, I suppose. As for the puddle-louper, it's lik drivin wi castors in yer erse.'

A SIGNALMAN who had worked for most of his career in the confines of a signalbox at Insch was due to retire after forty years' service. A presentation was arranged, much to his disgust, for he 'wintit nae nonsense'.

Handing over a cheque, the stationmaster said: 'Congratulations, Sam. Something of a railway record; forty years in one box.'

Sam's reply, head down with the words muttered from the side of his mouth, was: 'I'll be langer in the neist.'

IAN DAWSON, from Dyce, was known for his straight-faced stories and tells of the time he was in local government and attending council committee meetings.

A colleague was reminiscing on former councillors and asked how old one former acquaintance might be now as he hadn't seen him for ages.

'He's nae interactin wi his environment ony mair,' said Ian.

'Fit?'

'He's deid.'

IT WAS a postie in the Rosemount district of Aberdeen who made us wonder how many tales of the North-east are locked away in the minds of those who are now at the twilight of their lives, with no means of passing on these tales.

The postie in question was dealing with bulk mail,

the type that cannot be shoved through the confines of the letterbox, and he told us of delivering the regular book-club new editions of Mills & Boon to an old lady in Rosemount.

In her eighties, and of rural origin, he met her on the doorstep one delivery morning and asked if she still enjoyed reading all these romantic novels.

'Ach,' she said, 'I've been gettin them for years and I dinna wint tae stop noo. The only bits I dinna like are fin they start haulin the claes aff ccn anither.'

RONNIE WATSON, now retired to Dundee, recalls his Army days in North Africa in 1943. During an eerie lull in proceedings, he was looking round his exhausted comrades, bedraggled, wild-eyed and sore with the heat, when his mate Big Jake from Huntly, said: 'I dinna ken if Rommel's worried aboot this lot, bit they scare the buggery oot o me.'

Mixter Maxter

Not every story fits neatly into one of our subject headings, so here are all the odds and ends that we couldn't squeeze in anywhere else.

A BANFFSHIRE man who prefers not to be named told of his grandfather, who had recovered from a serious illness in the late 1950s and, having had one scare, thought he would like to make some arrangements for the future, so he went to the undertaker and explained he would like a coffin to keep in his shed, just so he could be sure that he would be laid away properly when his time came.

'We cwid mak ye een,' said the undertaker. 'Finest Oregon pine, polished brass plates, satin linins, silk tossles, fifty-one poun, the lot.'

'Michty, I wis doon at the jiner the ither day and he said he wid mak me a boxie for twinty poun.'

'Weel, g'awa til the jiner if ye please, bit I'll gie ye a fortnicht and yer erse'll be oot the dowp o't.'

IN THE early 1930s, an aunt of Helen Mills, now of Spey Bay, was maid to a Mrs Thompson at Braes of Enzie farm, near Buckie. One spring Sunday, on her day off, the maid picked an armful of catkins while walking by the River Spey, intending to use them as an arrangement she was doing for a special occasion for her mistress at the farm.

On her way home, she met Lily and Lizzie, two local quines also out for a walk.

'Oh, what bonnie pussy-willas,' said Lizzie. 'Fit are they for?'

'They're for a do at Mrs Thompson's,' said the maid.

As the two girls walked past, the maid heard Lily turn to Lizzie and mutter: 'I nivver kent doos ate catkins.'

The bargain boxie

THE ladies of one North-east golf club had signed up for a weekend outing to Spey Bay. For an extremely reasonable fee, they were entitled to return coach travel, a round of golf on the Saturday, an evening meal, entertainment, a night's accommodation, a hearty Scottish breakfast, another round of golf and lunch before heading home.

When Kath discovered that the entertainment was to be a popular band known as The Seagulls, she was delighted and could hardly wait for Saturday evening.

Fortified by a good meal and a sherry or two, Kath was sitting in the lounge tapping her feet and beaming at the musicians. She was apparently unaware that The Seagulls had had to call off at the last minute and had been replaced at short notice by another combo entirely.

This would not normally have caused any problem but, with the effect of the sherries, Kath decided to visit the loo between numbers. Walking past the band that she still imagined was The Seagulls, she grinned mischievously at the lead singer and inquired:

'Hiv ye poopit on onybody lately?'

BILL PIRIE was leading a group of novice hillwalkers along a particularly remote and tricky part of Glencoe when they were confronted with a ledge narrow enough to cause some of the participants a little concern.

Bill assured them that every precaution had been taken and that, as long as they didn't do anything silly, it was as safe as crossing the road.

'But just suppose een o's dis slip,' said one middle-aged woman. 'Fit should we dee?'

'Weel,' said Bill, 'the best thing wid be snappin yer heid as hard as ye can til the left.'

'Fit dis that dee, like?' asked the woman.

'It disna stop ye fa'in,' said Bill, 'bit what a rare view ye get on the wye doon.'

'Do ye ken the Birdie Song?'

WHEN THE film *Fatal Attraction* was released, queues built up outside the cinema in Aberdeen. One evening, Frances Robb was sitting engrossed in the story with two or three of her chums from work.

In the scene where Michael Douglas and Glenn Close were overcome with passion in the kitchen and began rolling from worktop to table to floor and back again, Frances said she became aware of the middle-aged couple in the row in front.

The woman leaned to the man and said: 'You nivver get workit up lik him.'

And the man leaned back and said: 'He gets peyed for't.'

IT'S SAD to see the decline in boatbuilding round our coast and the demise of the wooden-built hulls requiring special skills handed down through the generations.

It was the annual holiday at Turra and, with the usual closedown of all market-town activity, Jock and Aggie would 'hae a day oot' in the Austin 7 and headed for Buckie.

Once they had parked the motor, they would have a daunder round the harbour and stopped by Herd and Mackenzie's Yard, where work was in full swing.

The foreman took them in and was explaining one particular art as the caulker was hard at work. It was pointed out that the process, with the tradesman deftly hammering in the waterproof material, was to pack the seams between the planks of the bottom of the boat to prevent leakage.

Jock came up with the sensible suggestion:

'Wid it nae be easier pittin the boords closer thegither?'

A SLIP of the tongue from your co-author who is also a Highland Games commentator.

It was at Oldmeldrum Sports in June and a competitor made his debut having travelled all the way from the Isle of Arran to compete in the heavy events.

On introducing the young athlete as he threw the light hammer, over the Tannoy came:

'That was young Scott Clark throwing the hammer aa the wye fae the Isle of Arran.'

To which judge Bob Aitken retorted: 'Michty, Robbie, at's fairly a new record for Meldrum.'

WE WERE reminded of a tale going back to the days of the whaling by Bob Smith's excellent book *Buchan – Land of Plenty*.

There has always been great rivalry between the fishing ports of Fraserburgh and Peterhead. In the days of the whaling, Peterhead was making a name for itself with something like 30 whalers in the Arctic, well ahead of the tally from Fraserburgh.

Not to be outdone, a notice appeared at the Broch Harbour, proclaiming

HALF OF OUR WHALING FLEET SAILED YESTERDAY
THE OTHER HALF WILL LEAVE TOMORROW

What it didn't say was that half of the fleet was one ship; there were only two whalers sailing from the port.

SEVERAL years ago, when Aberdeen were playing an Italian side in a European football tournament, the usual exodus of supporters had driven, bussed and flown to Italy to roar on the Dons.

After the match, one forlorn supporter had been celebrating (or, more likely, drowning his sorrows) and had become detached from his party and had missed his flight.

In a haze of alcohol, he realised that the best course of action was to thumb a lift north to Turin where he might be able to convert his ticket for a later plane.

And so, still much the worse for wear, he came to be standing at the side of a rain-spattered autostrada, sticking out his thumb and hoping that someone would stop in time.

Eventually, a coach pulled in and our man, soaking jacket up around his ears, peered up at the driver as the door hissed open. Unknown to him, the coach was full of Dons supporters beginning their own long journey home.

'Eh, per favore,' said our man in halting Italian. 'Torino?'

'Sorry,' said the driver. 'Wid Bucksburn be ony eese?'

ON A VISIT in 1996 to Dingwall to record a programme for Radio Scotland's *Take the Floor* your presenter of that medium sought refuge after rehearsal in a wee pub in the centre of the town.

He was surprised to find only three people at the bar counter; a couple of Gaelic teuchters and a gentleman the waur o the weer who spoke with a real North-east tongue.

Ordering a refreshing lager, Robbie must have given away by his tongue that he was of the North-east and this was richt inta the barra of the gentleman, who turned out to be a retired farmer from the Howe o Cromar.

After regaling the wee company with a lecture on the Doric, in the Doric, his two pals started conversing in Gaelic to wind him up.

'Ach,' snapped Mr Douneside, 'pey nae attention; I've tellt them afore the Doric's jist as important as their yab-yab-yabble in the Gaelic.'

Then he turned on his two companions. 'Listen til es, you twa. If it wisna for fowk lik me, and fowk lik him,' – pointing to Robbie, whom he didn't recognise – 'and if it wisna for Robbie Shepherd, the Doric wid be deid.'

OVERHEARD AT Lawrence of Kemnay, an enthusiastic salesman was dealing with a chary client.

'Parliamo Doric?'

'And I suppose,' said the customer, 'that ye'll tell me, lik ivry ither car salesman, that it's jist hid ae careful owner?'

'Ay,' said the salesman, adding with admirable honesty, 'and a half-dizzen ither haimmerin buggers.'

THE LATE John Stammers, for long Registrar of Births, Deaths and Marriages at Braemar, often told this story against himself.

The wife of one of the village hotel managers, not native of Deeside, had given birth to a daughter, and the father approached John about registering the birth.

Our Braemar registrar asked what the child's name was to be and was told: 'Tamara.'

A bit nonplussed, John replied: 'Och aye, Tamara will dee fine. Fit time?'

JAMES SLATER, a Buckie fisherman, aye maintained that he had managed to get English classified as a foreign language when he did his National Service in the Royal Engineers.

At his interview on joining the Army, he was asked if he spoke any foreign tongue.

He replied: 'Ay, English.'

'What is your native tongue?' he was asked.

'Doric. It's spoken in North-east Scotland.'

He was lectured and told that regional accents were not separate languages, but James was thrawn and challenged the corporal.

They agreed that if he said something in Doric and the corporal did not understand what he said, the NCO would have English entered as a foreign language on his record and get the pay supplement for having an extra language.

Put to the test, James launched immediately into: 'Gin I hiv till eese a graip tae shuffle sharn an dubs for mony a wikk, I'll ca ee the feelest gype wi a gey clarty doup at ivver I clappit een on.'

He got his pay supplement.

IT APPEARS that all Observer Corps stations round the Granite City were on a party line connected with Centre and everybody listened in. Centre reminded all observers that they must report every aircraft. So it was that this conversation drew many a chuckle from those on duty.

'Newtonhull here. Spitfire, bearing 270, height sax fit, gyan north, over.'

'Centre here. Are you sure? Over.'

'Newtonhull replyin. Aye, over.'

'Centre here. Check co-ordinates again in two minutes, over.'

'Newtonhull here. Spitfire bearing 271. Height sax fit, proceeding north, over.'

'Centre here. He's impossibly slow. Check again, over.'

'Newtonhull here. He's nae that slow; jist on the back o a larry, oot.'

WE GO BACK to the days of few cars and fewer tourists. The usual gathering of locals had assembled in the middle of Cornhill when a fancy open-topped motor car screeched to a halt and the occupant beckoned the town worthy Frankie to come hither.

Neither Frankie nor anyone else moved. Further beckoning had no effect and the toff shouted in an irritated voice: 'Are you deaf, man? Does this road go to Portsoy?'

'Na,' said Frankie, hands in pockets, 'it bides here.'

A MEMBER of the Lonach Pipe Band recalled taking exception to a Strathdon laird who had been heard to say in a speech at some function that 'Life has been made very much more difficult in recent weeks by those pipe bands.'

Who knows what war might have broken out if someone else had not worked out that what the laird had actually said was:

'Life has been made very much more difficult in recent weeks by hosepipe bans.'

THE WHOLE village of Dunecht used to turn out for the travelling cinema shows in the village hall. The blinds would shut and the whirr of the projector would send a sense of great expectation round the assembly.

Aggie was a weel-kent and weel-liked craiter, but she was just a wee bit backward intellectually. She had seldom been anywhere out of the village and fair enjoyed the weekly treat at the makeshift cinema.

They happened to be showing *Old Mother Riley* one particular week and Aggie's guffaws of laughter soon had every head in the hall turning.

During one particular scene, where Ma Riley went straight through a strae-rick on her motorbike, Aggie, overcome by the drama of it all, jumped to her feet and ran back up the hall howling: 'Goadalmichty!'

THE FOLLOWING week, it was a Roy Rogers picture. The hero had just been shot and, to all intents and purposes, appeared dead. Having checked to make sure he was dead, the villain was about to leave the saloon when Roy rallied and started to rise.

Aggie, so mightily relieved to see that he was alive after all, and petrified in case the baddie would look back, skirled: 'Lie doon, Roy, ye feel bugger!'

IT HAS been rumoured, but never confirmed, that the recording mannie of the two of us had his car broken into recently.

His radio was gone, as were tapes of the Beatles and Oasis, his son's favourites, and his wife's easy-listening cassettes. Left behind were cassettes of himself belting out his bothy ballads.

The police are still looking for someone with an ear for music.

A FRASERBURGH skipper took his crew to a harbourside hostelry at the end of a successful trip because he wanted to stand his hand. On asking everyone what they would like, he found that each one replied: 'A pint wid dee fine.'

All except Tommy, who was reputed, literally, to have a very big mouth.

'Weel, Tom, and fit aboot you?'

'Ach, skipper, I'll jist hae a moofae.'

'Damn the linth, ye'll tak a pint lik a'body else.'

The Tales that Got Awa

Once again, here are the stories which arrived in the mail and which didn't have quite the same ring of truth as all the others. They were too good to waste, though. With the customary warning that you enter this section at your own risk, go ahead.

A MAN visited his GP complaining of a severe rash across his back which seemed to be spreading and was maddeningly itchy. The GP examined him and was aghast at what he found. 'You're suffering from a severe form of jungle contagion,' he told his patient.

'Is that serious like, doctor?'

'Well, it tends to spread very quickly – twenty-four hours is about the limit of it – and three-quarters of cases result in a painful, agonising death.'

The patient swallowed hard. 'Michty, doctor, is there nae cure?'

The doctor thought for a moment. 'G'awa ben the corridor,' he said, 'and lock yersel intil that wee roomie at the eyn. We'll pit ye on a special diet o Ryvita and Kraft cheese slices.'

'And will that cure me?'

'No, bit it's a' we can slide aneth the door.'

AN AMERICAN woman on holiday in Aberdeen was being driven round the city when the car had to stop at a pelican crossing. The crossing began its usual peeping.

'Say, what's that noise?' she inquired of her host.

'Oh, that's the noise so that blind people know when the crossing's active.'

'Gee,' said the American woman, 'in the States, we don't let blind people drive cars.'

AN ELDERLY North-east couple owned a holiday cottage which they let out during summers. One summer, the husband discovered that the family who had rented it were nudists and had been cavorting in privacy behind the hedges in their birthday suits.

The old man was alarmed that the neighbours might find out, or even call the police, so he rushed home to tell his wife.

'Ye'll nivver guess, Jeannie,' he said, breathless. 'Fit div ye think they're using the craftic for?'

She shook her head.

'A nudist bare-nakit setoot. Not a stitch. Oh, Jeannie, fit'll we dee?'

Jeannie thought for a moment. 'There's jist ae thing we can dee,' she said.

'Fit's that?'

'Double their rent.'

THE WOMAN who owned the village craft shop went storming into the butcher to complain that the lamb chops she had bought the previous Saturday had shrunk so much in the pan that they were hardly worth the bother of cooking and serving.

'Well, if we're hearin complaints,' said the butcher, 'ye're as weel kennin that yon jersey I bocht fae ye for ma wife's birthday shrunk sae muckle in the wash that it widna even fit ma dother's dollie noo.'

'Weel,' said another customer, who had been listening intently, 'I doot the chops and the oo come aff the same lambie.'

BERTIE REID was a steady smoker and his wife had had no luck in trying to get him to stop, so she tried shaming him into quitting.

'Bertie,' she said, 'Alfie Duncan doon the road, he's stoppit smokin. Foo's that for willpower, eh? That's a rale man, if ye ask me. Stoppit smokin jist lik that. Willpower.'

Alfie stood up. 'I'll show ye willpower,' he said, and for the next seven weeks he slept alone in the spare room.

Mrs Reid took it in good part at first, but she missed Bertie at night. Finally, one night she tiptoed to the spare room, opened the door slightly and whispered:

'Bertie? Are ye sleepin, Bertie? Alfie Duncan's startit smokin again.'

AN ELDERLY woman crofter not a million miles from Foggieloan won the WRI monthly competition for redcurrant jelly and was given a choice of prize. She could have had a felt hat made by a fellow-member, or she could have had a straw hat made by the same woman.

'I'll tak the straa hat,' said the winner after hardly any deliberation at all.

'Fit wye did ye tak the straa hattie?' enquired the hatmaker later. 'The felt hat cost twice the price and took near double the time ti pit thegiether.'

'Aweel,' said the elderly winner, 'the felt hattie wis bonnie, richt eneuch, bit the straa hattie's better for me. Fin it's ca'ed deen, I can feed it til the nowt.'

THANKS TO the Kennethmont reader who sent us this story. We're not sure that this is tasteful enough for the book, so those of a nervous disposition should turn the page.

She claims that while she was a nurse at Inverurie Hospital, not long after it had become an exclusively geriatric unit, she had been accompanying a doctor who was attending a sad old craiter who had just been admitted and whose prognosis was not good.

'Tell me,' said the doctor kindly, 'have you ever been bedridden before?'

'Oh, aye,' said the old lady. 'Mony a time. And twice in the back o a cairt.'

'Gweed eneuch ti aet'

ECHT SHOW was wearing to a close and Sandy had spent just a little too long in the beer tent with his cronies. Out in the fresh air, the warm whisky was taking its toll and he started making his weary way home on foot.

The road and the ditches seemed to merge and he stumbled off the side of the road up to his waist in water.

Striding out of that as best he could, he continued his journey and was relieved to find a telephone box on his road home to Midmar.

Dialling his wife, he said: 'Sorry, quine. It's been a fairish day. I've jist faan intil a ditch. Can ye come for me?'

'Bit far are ye ringin fae?'

'Fae the erse doon.'

THERE WERE not that many phone calls to the household of Jock and Sadie in their cottage by the farm on the road ben the seashore by the Broch – at least not when Jock was at home.

He would often have business with his float to uptail and ca the nowt from some particular mart, which meant an early start.

So it was that the phone rang one morning with Jock, for once, enjoying the extra snooze before rising time.

Jock hirpled, pyjama trousers nearly tripping him up, to the phone downstairs.

Upstairs, Sadie could hear Jock's muffled: 'Hello? Hello?', followed by an expletive or two.

Sleepy-eyed Jock crept back up the stair to be greeted with an anxious: 'Fa wis 'at?'

'Ach,' he said. 'A wrang number. Some fisher billie, I doot, for he wis speirin gin the coast wis clear.'

EVERY NEW Year, the telephone lines become red hot as far-off and near-at-hand relations get into sentimental mood. A Guid New Year is sung again and again, and promptly forgotten in the subsequent sober moments of the day.

Tam was not one of those revellers. He liked his bawbees too much to spend on such ploys. However, the phone did ring at four one New Year's morning and it was Tam who was kicked out of bed to answer the call.

His anxious wife – thinking, at that time of the morning, that a close relative might have passed away – prodded Tam as he crept back into bed.

'Fa wis't? Aathing aa richt?'

Tam grunted.

'Some damnt gype sayin it wis a lang distance fae Australia. Ony feel kens at. I jist clappit doon the phone on him.'

A FARMER from Auchnagatt was instructed by his wife to nip in past Duncan Fraser's when he was in town and get her a new bra for a forthcoming farmers' ball.

On arriving at the requisite counter, he was asked which size?

'Oh lassie, I dinna ken muckle aboot sic things.'

'But you know the size of your wife, surely. Any idea at all?'

He scratched his head for a minute or two, then ventured: 'Size thirteen.'

'Thirteen?' said the assistant. 'Surely not. How do you arrive at that?'

'Weel,' he said, 'my bonnet's sax and sivven-eichths and it haps jist een o them.'

AN UNIDENTIFIED Deeside woman told us of a Mrs Brown from a village up Deeside. Mrs Brown is supposedly a traditionalist and bemoans the demise of more and more of the local grocers' shops. Her own village shop is still on the go, but changes must be made to keep up with the big stores.

On entering the shop recently, she asked for her usual
'steen o tatties'.

'Sorry,' said Alex from behind the counter. 'We dinna sell
that ony mair. It's kilos noo.'

'Ach weel,' she said, 'jist gie's a steen o kilos.'

IT SEEMS that most infant and nursery teachers keep spare
clothes in case of accidents at school with all the excitement
of the early days of lessons.

One wee girl at a Fraserburgh primary unfortunately had
such an accident and wet her pants. The teacher dutifully
changed the wee lass and sent the wet pair home in a plastic
carrier bag.

You can imagine the commotion in the bus the next day
when wee Lee-Anne, sitting with her father, spotted the
teacher at the front.

In a loud voice, the wee lass said:

'Miss MacGregor, my dad's got your knickers in his
pooch.'

THREE YOUNG lads from around the Cruden Bay area
were in a huddle one day discussing their respective fathers
and venturing as to which dad would be the bravest.

'My faither's affa brave,' said Tam. 'He saw twa robbers
comin oot o the Clydesdale Bunk at Peterheid and he
rugby-tackelt them baith, haudin them doon till the bobbies
arrived. Aye, my dad's the bravest.'

'Na, na,' said John. 'My dad heard o somebody that hid
faan doon the cliffs o the Bullers o Buchan. Athoot a safety
harness or onything, he gaed doon the brae face and bade
there directin the helicopters. My dad's the bravest.'

But Willie was silent.

'Fit aboot you, Willie?' they asked.

'Na,' said Willie sadly. 'My faither's a cooard.'

'Fit wye?'

'Ilky time ma mither's awa seein ma unty in Edinburgh

for the wikkend, he needs the wifie in fae next door tae sleep wi him.'

EVEN AS late as the 1960s, neighbouring farmers round the Garioch used to take it in turns to host entertainments for their friends.

Hilly came into the kitchen where his wife was preparing the goodies for the forthcoming party. She was looking somewhat doon in the moo, and hubby asked what was wrong.

'Ach,' said Jean. 'It's this trifle. I hinna ony o yon silver ballies that Bogie's wife hid on her een last year.'

'Nivver fash,' said the loving husband. 'I'll jist teem a cartridge ower the heid o't and naebody'll be ony the wiser.'

The night of the party came and went and, next morning, Hilly was calling in past his neighbours to see how things were doing.

'Weel, Mains, hid ye a gweed time last nicht?'

Ay, man, it wis a grand affair. Jist ae thing. The wife wis haulin on her draaers this mornin and she shot the cat.'

Glossary

Anither guide to the Doric as she is spak

Aeten	Eaten
Aneth	Beneath, below
Auler	Older
Barrafaes	Barrowloads
Bathert	Bothered
Beets	Boots
Ben	Through
Bide	Stay
Blaad	Damage, spoil
Bocht	Bought
Bosie	Embrace, hug, cuddle
Brakk	Break
Breein	Straining water from
Bugfae	Bagful
Ca nowt	Transport cattle
Caafies	Calves
Ca'ed deen	Worn out
Cairt	Cart
Claes	Clothes
Claikin	Gossiping
Clarty	Dirty
Coo'ard	Coward

Coorse	Bad
Craiters	Creatures
Cubbidge	Cabbage
Cuttie	Pipe
Cwidna	Could not
Deemie	Young woman
Dicht	Wipe
Dipper	Tank for sheep-dipping
Dizzen	Dozen
Doon in the moo	Depressed, out of sorts
Dother	Daughter
Dowp, Doup	Backside, posterior
Drookit	Drenched
Dubs	Mud
Dungars	Overalls, dungarees
Dyeucks	Duck
Eese	Use
Eest tae	Used to
Eneuch	Enough
Eyn	End
Faan, faun	Fallen
Far	Where
Fash	Trouble, perturb
Feart	Afraid

Feel	Stupid
Ficher	Fumble
File	While
Fit wye	Why
Folly	Follow
Foo	How
Grieve	Foreman, farm-worker
Gype	Idiot, poltroon (usu. male)
Haps	Covers
Haud gyan	Keep going
Haulin	Pulling
Hich	High
Hirpled	Hobbled
Hoo'er	Prostitute (or unpleasant (adj.))
Ilka, ilky	Every
Ingins	Onions
Interficherin	Interfering with
Intimmers	(anat.) Insides
Ivnoo	Now, at this moment
Larry	Lorry
Lees	Lies
Linth	Length
Loon	Boy
Louper	Jumper

Louse	Loose
Lowsin time	End of day's work
Moofae	Mouthful
Nae wye	Nowhere
Neen	None
Neep	Turnip
Neist	Next
Nivver fash	Don't worry
Nowt	Cattle
Oo	Wool
Orraman	Farm labourer
Pish	Urinate
Ploo	Plough
Pooch	Pocket
Raivelt	Confused
Rale	Real
Raxin	Stretching
Reid hett	Red hot
Rickle	Pile, haphazard collection
Roch grun	Rough ground
Rodden	Rowan
Sair grun	Barren land
Satty	Salty
Scutter	Delay

Semmit & draa'ers	Vest and pants
Sharn	Slurry
Shooed	Sewed, sewn
Siller	Money, cash
Skelpit	Smacked
Skyte	Slide
Sook	Suck
Soon	Sound
Soss	Mess
Souter	Shoemaker
Speirin	Asking
Spunks	Matches, lucifers
Stammick	Stomach
Stammygaster	Astonishment
Steen	Stone
Steen caul	Stone cold
Straa	Straw
Strae-rick	Stack of straw
Stravaigin	Wandering, exploring
Taakin	Engaging
Teem	Empty
Tidee	Commotion
Tirred	Undressed
Toonsers	Indigenes of Aberdeen (derog.)

Trump	Tramp, step
Tyauve	Struggle (pron. 'chaav')
Waur o the weer	Worse for wear
Wheepit	Whipped
Win	Get
Wug	Wave
Wye	Way

Where Credit's Due

Once again, we can take hardly any of the credit for the stories you have read in the book. Many have come from our daily activities in newspapers and on the radio, but just as many arrived by post from fowk across the North-east, throughout the rest of the country, ay, and a dozen or so from the far-flung corners of the globe, forbye. To the best of our knowledge, they are true, apart from those we have flagged up clearly as wee works of fiction. We thank everyone who took the time and trouble to write to us, and especially the ones who said that they liked the first book. We feel we can at least record these contributions, whether we had the space to use them or not, so please accept our thanks. If we have missed out anyone in the hurry to get the book ready, we're sorry.

Thanks to Alison Harper, Esma Shepherd, John Duff, Ian Middleton, Johnnie Duncan, T. Munro Forsyth, Douglas Schaske, Christine Birnie, Ethel Baird, Doug Hampton, Geordie Stott, the Rev. Jim Scott, Jimmie Mitchell, Charles Barron, V.B. Taylor, R.P. Nicol, A.J. Harper, Mabel Mutch, James Morrison, Frances Patterson, Duncan Downie, Leslie and Hilda Innes, Kenny Mackie, Donald Manson, Norman Harper sen., Joan Christie, Ethel Simpson, Nan Sandison, Douglas Mutch, Lilianne Grant Rich, Rena Gaiter, Bill Mathers, Gordon Milne, Graham Maclennan, Chrissabel Reid, John Stewart, Mrs M. Riddoch, Bob Knowles, Andrew Foster, Bill Connon, H. Walker, Isobel and Peter Slater, Douglas Merson, Norah Hardy, Violet Thomson, Yvonne Cormack, Jess Robertson, Donald McAllister, Jim Glennie, J.O. McHardy, Elizabeth Hendry, Willie Smith, Bill Mowat, Elma Massie, Ian Dawson, Ronnie Watson, Helen Mills, Bill Pirie, Frances Robb, Janice Cottier, Nicholas and Cameron Harper, Jim McColl, Mary Gerrie, Eric Wilson, Karen Buchan, Nanny and Hilda, Joe Watson, John Dear,

George Durward, David Ross, Eileen Dunn, Sheila Innes, Jimmy Lees, Dr Pat Macdonald, Jimmy Irvine, Bill Shand, Kathie Ross, the Rev. Gordon Smith, the Rev. Charles Birnie, Margaret Mathison, Sandy Matheson, Frances Jaffray, Sandy Watt, Lorna Alexander and dozens of others who wrote and requested anonymity, as well as thousands who, over the years, have entertained us with their conversation.

Robbie Shepherd and Norman Harper
Aberdeen, 1996